IN THE COMPANY OF A SIDDHA

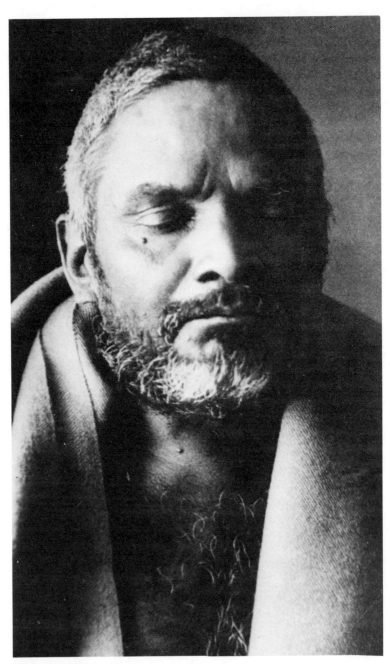

BHAGAWAN NITYANANDA

Everything you seek is within you.
If you want to become happy, then go within,
because happiness lies within you.
And if you are seeking love, then seek it within,
because love also lies within you.
God has stored everything inside you.

—Swami Muktananda

IN THE
COMPANY
OF A
SIDDHA

*Interviews and Conversations
with Swami Muktananda*

PUBLISHED BY S.Y.D.A. FOUNDATION, OAKLAND, CALIFORNIA

LCCN: 78-65085 ISBN 0-914602-46-9

Credits: Edited and narrated by Karen (Kalyani) Alboher
Front and back cover photos courtesy of Krishna Dharma Lowe.
Other photos courtesy of Gauri Hubert, Lee Whitehead, and Krishna Dharma Lowe.

CONTENTS

INTRODUCTION .

My first encounter with Swami Muktananda occurred at a reception in his honor near Stanford University soon after his arrival in San Francisco in April, 1974. The invited guests were scientists, therapists, educators and other professionals who were researching altered states of consciousness or working with that mysterious nonphysical energy of a thousand different names. Muktananda's name for it, I was soon to learn, was Shakti.

As a Reichian therapist, I too, had been actively dealing with this life-force energy, which I referred to as *orgone*. As a founder of an Esalen-type growth center, I worked closely with many of the leaders in the consciousness movement. At the time I was even working on a book that surveyed all the many disciplines, old and new, which had their own approach to this energy. I had sampled some fifty of these disciplines in my research, including Bioenergetics, Acupuncture, Vivaxis, Polarity Therapy, Radiesthesia, Theosophy, and Psychic Healing. I was reluctant to look at any more, but I had agreed to meet this man called a Siddha yogi, or a perfect Master.

On the drive home after the reception and lecture, my friends and I got into an animated discussion about the need to surrender to a guru if one were to benefit from his teaching. My friends were quite knowledgeable about the subject, but I didn't know the first thing about gurus and had definitely not been seeking one. Muktananda was the first one I had met. I was surprised to feel a jolt of fear run through me as they argued the necessity of surrender. To me it just meant being at the mercy of someone.

Puzzled over my reaction, I decided to go with my friends to visit Muktananda at his Ashram in Piedmont. At the first opportunity I told him about my fear of surrendering to him. He told me that among his followers were many people in government and the professions who still retained their posts. He reassured me that, like the river which flows into the sea, I had nothing to lose and much to gain. I saw that, in fact, I was only focusing on what I might lose and not at all on what I might gain from contact with him. After the meeting was over, he bounded out of his chair, came over to me, put his arm around my shoulder, and rubbed my chest with his hand. I was a little startled.

After that, I found myself being drawn toward him and his Ashram as if by a magnetic force. I did not have a single clear-cut dramatic Shaktipat experience, but I obviously had received his "touch," which was working subtly on me. I attended all of his lectures in the Bay Area. I began to visit him frequently, and I even got up at 4:30 a.m. to attend his morning meditation sessions. I was getting quite a bit from him: impressive meditation experiences, steadily increasing energy, and a warm, supportive relationship.

It was not long before I tried living in his Ashram, and I traveled with him for a while. When he left the Bay Area for New York in March of 1976, I remained behind and eventually re-established my private practice. Almost two years elapsed before I saw him again in December of 1977, when I visited his Ashram in India for a couple of months.

In my relationship with Muktananda I have been a participant-observer under varying conditions: being with him for short and long periods, living in his Ashram with and without him, and living away from him. He has tested me, and I have tested him through direct, deep, and long-term experience. The net-result of my four-year relationship with Muktananda has been a deep transformation of my way of being, relating, and working. It has convinced me that Muktananda's teachings really work.

Baba's message to the world is simple and terse: "Meditate on the Self. God is within you as you." It is the first sutra of his Siddha Yoga. The meaning and significance of meditation and the Self are to be found in them as he describes and explains them to all kinds of people.

What can not come across explicitly in this kind of book, however, is the key role of the teacher. As a therapist, I knew how vital the therapist-patient relationship was in the healing process—far more than any particular technique used. And I knew there was a guru-disciple relationship in yoga. But I was unprepared for the great emphasis put on this relationship in Siddha Yoga. "The guru is the means," says an aphorism in the spiritual philosophy of Kashmir Shaivism. And so he is. Everything in Siddha Yoga revolves around Muktananda.

To understand why this is so, we must look at the role of the guru. A guru has a three-fold function. First, he is here to teach us divine love and to love ourselves as well as others. Second, he is here to teach us how to get off the time-wheel of cause and effect (*karma*) by acting in the world with detachment. Third, he is here to help us to become established in constant awareness or witness-consciousness, and thus united with universal Consciousness.

It has often been said that the central question of the spiritual quest is: "Who am I?" This is so on the Siddha Path as well. However, since the relationship to the guru is so vital on this path, there is a corollary that must be asked of Muktananda: "Who are you?" A great deal of time is spent in looking at him, thinking about him, in essence, meditating on him. This does not deflect, as one might think, from the pursuit of understanding "Who am I?" In fact, the effort to understand Muktananda leads to greater understanding of oneself. "Who are you?" naturally leads back to "Who am I?" The ultimate answer to both questions is the same—the Self. Muktananda's continual reflection of the Self is evident, and provides easier access to our own Self.

Just who is Muktananda? Much has been said about his God-realization, which I will take up shortly. First, I want to stress his human-realization. What impressed me most about him at the outset is his mastery of an extraordinary number of talents, interests, and abilities. He is a musician, a vocalist, a "choir" (chanting) conductor. He is a master cook. He is a businessman and economist, the administrator of his Ashram and organizer of his tours. He is a yogi, a guru, a saint. He is a poet, a writer, a lecturer. He is a practical teacher as well as a philosophy teacher. He has been an Ayurvedic physician. His prodigious talents make me think of men of the Renaissance. Nowadays, such diverse abilities are rarely found in one and the same person. Moreover, it is most unusual for a Self-realized yogi to be so much at home in the workaday world. Here is someone to model oneself after—someone who is both practical and theoretical, both materialistic and spiritual.

As a long-time student of character and personality, I gave a lot of thought to Muktananda's. I saw him be loving. I saw him be fiercely angry. I saw him be mischievous. I saw him be compassionate. I saw him cry in public. He seemed to me to be one of the most natural, unself-conscious individuals I had ever met. He was utterly devoid of any posing or artificiality. He just didn't seem to have any ego. He functioned out of the moment. All of this made him a very alive, unpredictable, and human human being.

As a therapist, I could not help but see Muktananda and his Ashram in therapeutic terms. Living in his Ashram, under the pressure of discipline and close living and working conditions, I observed people consciously or unconsciously working through deep hang-ups in their personalities. I saw many have corrective emotional experiences which led to better relating, and it seemed to be happening spontaneously—the Shakti was causing it, while Muktananda was always in the background as a supportive father-figure. I once remarked jokingly to him that it appeared he was putting therapists out of work.

On another level, Muktananda is a master of life-force energy, or Shakti. He can give powerful "injections" of it just by a mere touch or look. Not to a few, but to thousands. He seems to be an inexhaustible powerhouse of it. Not only can he transmit this Shakti to others and bring about an inner awakening in them (Shaktipat), but he can guide and control this energy whenever necessary. Moreover, he is able to build it up and maintain it in buildings, so that former night clubs and flophouse hotels can be transformed into temples vibrating with this energy. Modern devices, such as orgone boxes, samadhi tanks, pyramids, and the like, can hardly compare to his meditation rooms. Similarly, a weekend with him in an Intensive is super-charged when he transfers his energy directly through Shaktipat. And it is even more dynamic on his home ground in Ganeshpuri. His Shakti is the open secret behind the power of his mantra to give instant experiences of the Self.

After I found myself getting so involved with Muktananda, I read omnivorously about yoga; not just the familiar classics, but also those he recommended, which are unknown in the West. I learned that there are a great many kinds of yoga. Different seekers require different paths to the Absolute: love (*bhakti*), knowledge (*jnana*), or service (*karma*). There are other paths based on the various techniques used, such as harnessing the mind (*raja*) and repetition of holy syllables (*mantra*). And still others are based on some aspect, such as latent energy *(Kundalini)* or inner visions and sounds *(laya)*. A yogi is ordinarily expert in only a couple of these after many years of dedicated practice. Muktananda, as a Siddha, is knowledgeable and skillful in all of them. They manifest in him as needed. His versatility attracts a wide range of seekers, and as they pursue the path of Siddha Yoga, knowledge of these various yogas arises spontaneously within them.

Finally, there is the matter—the most crucial matter of all—of his being permanently established in the highest state of consciousness, of his being one with the witness, one with universal Consciousness. For a long time I could not truly experience what this meant. His multiple psychic powers, such as knowing people's thoughts and the future, are evidence that his consciousness is not ordinary. But these are minor powers, whereas being one with universal Consciousness is a transcendant psychic power that seems to carry with it a moral imperative—it functions only for the greatest good, furthering the spiritual development of his disciples. Understanding this aspect of Muktananda takes one into a realm that is beyond psychotherapy. In psychotherapy only the contents of the mind are examined, not the mind itself. In order for me to comprehend his state at all, there had to be a change in the structure of my mind. As I gained some semblance of witness-consciousness myself, I was then able to experience him, and also the world, differently.

But Muktananda is only part of this relationship—the guru. What about the disciple? Disciples come in a wide range of types. There is not space to adequately describe them. It must suffice to mention a few traits that are particularly important. Most significant is a deep longing to penetrate the meaning of one's existence. Also important are a keen intelligence to understand the subtle way the guru works and a willingness to endure the discipline that is required. A Siddha does not make any decision about accepting someone as a disciple. Muktananda accepts all comers. It is the disciple's decision whether to enter into a relationship or not. Muktananda responds individually to each disciple and thus every relationship is uniquely suited to the disciple's needs and potentialities. The disciple has in Muktananda the many-aspected figure I described, and he will relate to whatever aspect attracts him. It is a relationship that can go deep—very deep—because it involves the relationship with divinity. Muktananda is committed to seeing his disciple through to the perfection of his spiritual practice; so it all depends on the disciple how far and how fast he goes. If the disciple can hang in there, the relationship with the Siddha Guru will result in a complete transformation of his life, both inner and outer.

The guru-disciple relationship is the pillar on which Siddha Yoga rests, yet Muktananda does use a few teaching devices or techniques. The unusual effectiveness of these few techniques really stems from Muktananda and his Shakti. The techniques are meditation, mantra repetition, and chanting. These are the day-in, day-out practices that Muktananda stresses to purify the body, the mind, and the ego. He describes the procedures for and value of engaging in these practices in the following pages.

There is a fourth method of teaching—one that was not usually identified as such—but one that caught my psychologist's eye. That was *darshan*. In India to have someone's *darshan* traditionally means seeing or being near a saint or a great being. It is a mysterious procedure that was considered to bring good luck, and with Muktananda it can also be the occasion for the subtle transference of Shakti. His mere presence can act as a catalyst for an opening into the Self. Having Muktananda's *darshan* was a daily feature of life in his Ashram, and these *darshans* came in several different forms. There were large formal gatherings for the general public in which one might have a brief contact with him and in which he answered general questions and also gave lectures. In contrast were the rare private *darshans* in which one could be alone with him for a very personal, intimate talk. In between were the "semi-private" *darshans* in which one could talk about one's spiritual or mundane problems in the presence of a small group. These semi-private *darshans* also provided an opportunity for visitors to engage in in-depth dialogues with Muktananda. The visitor could be a writer doing an interview on a particular subject, a celebrity in the consciousness literary scene, a scientist researching psychic phenomena, or a well-known spiritual leader. Muktananda enjoyed such conversations and so did the others present. I attended many of these *darshans* and also invited several of my colleagues to come and have discussions with Muktananda. The conversations from these special *darshans* form the heart of this book. It is indeed fortunate that one disciple, Kalyani, had the foresight and perseverance to take them down in shorthand and later to compile and edit them for this book.

These dialogues permit one to see Muktananda's personality in action. They reveal his genuine interest in people and his ability to converse with all kinds, no matter what their background. With little formal education, he evidences a tremendous breadth of knowledge in a wide range of subjects. But no matter how interested he is in the subject and no matter how much he talks at the level of the interviewer, he always comes back to his essential teaching: "Meditate on the Self."

A point that Muktananda keeps making throughout many of these dialogues is the necessity of having direct, personal experience with higher states of consciousness and spiritual energy. This may seem obvious but it is easy to forget this simple truth. Again and again, he exhorts the scientist to study himself, the healer to heal himself, the psychologist to witness his own mind. The pressures to achieve and perform in these fields before one has gone very far into one's own Self are very great in America. Muktananda says that the journey into the Self can only make one into a better therapist, a better minister, a better researcher. Nothing will be lost; much will be gained. That is what he told me when I first met him. From direct, personal experience I have found that he was speaking the truth.

I see Muktananda as a human-realized being, a master of nonphysical energy, a perfect yogi and a God-realized being. Some may feel that no such human being could exist, but my portrait of him is not exaggerated. He truly is a formidable figure to relate to. He is more like a force than a human being.

Harold S. Streitfeld
Oakland, California
May, 1978

1
MUKTANANDA
MEETS THE PRESS

Wherever Swami Muktananda goes, he encounters reporters. They come from big city newspapers and major television stations as well as from spiritual magazines and public interest radio stations. Unlike most of the visitors who come to see the Guru, few of these reporters have much interest in meditation or yoga. They respond to him on a purely human level, appreciating his humor and enjoying the mysteriously joyful atmosphere that surrounds him. "I don't know what's going on here, but I'm sure having a good time!" said a television reporter in his on-camera commentary after interviewing Muktananda in the courtyard of his Ashram in Oakland, California. When Muktananda asked a photographer from a big New York City paper if he would like to have some coffee, the man answered, "I don't drink coffee, but I'll have some if you want me to. You make me happy, so I'd like to make you happy."

Part of what intrigues media people about Baba Muktananda is his unpredictability, the spontaneity with which he turns a routine encounter into something magical. Once, in New York, an NBC camera crew came to shoot a news sequence on Muktananda. After the interview, the director asked Baba if they could film him taking his daily walk through the countryside near the DeVille Ashram. Muktananda agreed and set off immediately, followed by a cameraman, a soundman, and the director. As he passed through the lobby of the DeVille, he kept beckoning people to come along, and as one devotee after another joined in, the walk began to look like a parade. "Are you sure this is the way you usually walk?" the director asked. "We want it to look normal."

When the request was translated, Baba nodded as if understanding had finally dawned, and then turned to the crowd following him. "All right," he said, "nobody should look at the camera!" At this, the director broke into helpless laughter. The procession continued for a few minutes, but then Muktananda sent the devotees away and set off on the solitary stroll the director had had in mind. But her ideas about Gurus, she later confessed, were never the same again.

Swami Muktananda has as many ways of teaching as there are situations in which to teach, and virtually everyone who comes into his presence receives some lesson in the process. Often, press interviews would turn into personal interviews, with the reporter asking for advice or personal guidance. Sometimes Muktananda would give his mantra or touch the reporter on the forehead and ask him to sit quietly for awhile. One of the most unusual of these spontaneous initiations occurred in Miami, Florida, during a TV talk show. The host was asking about initiation by physical touch, and at last he asked. "If you touched me right now, would I experience inner peace?"

Muktananda explained that the touch is generally given in a special environment, under conditions suitable for the transmission of spiritual energy, but that people who receive it do experience inner peace. Then the host asked, "Would you touch me?" His interest was so clearly genuine that Muktananda responded by signaling him to come closer. He brushed him between the eyebrows and blew air into his nostrils. In that moment, despite the bright lights and the theatrical surroundings and the huge at-home viewing audience, Muktananda and the talk show host were simply those archetypal figures: the Guru and the seeker. The host leaned back in his chair, a stunned expression on his face. "I'm already feeling better," he said.

Muktananda advised, "When you go home tonight, sit quietly. This touch will not go to waste; it will affect you later in the night." The next day, the host telephoned Muktananda to thank him and said that he had, in fact, experienced a profound sense of inner peace that night.

Like other people who meet Muktananda, many journalists find that even brief contacts with him alter their lives. A reporter in Honolulu left her job to travel with him on tour, and she remained as a member of his staff. A writer in San Francisco was so fascinated after his initial interview with the Swami that he spent the next five months hanging out in his entourage; later, he wrote a book about his experiences. Journalists return again and again to spend time in Muktananda's presence. They meditate regularly and repeat his mantra, and they report that their sense of themselves is different since they have known him.

Most of the journalists who write about Muktananda share one difficulty: they find it next to impossible to capture his special qualities in print. They describe his movements, his personal style, the trademarks of his appearance—the dark glasses, the orange silks, the caps and socks which he invariably wears—and they report what he says and does. But they find that descriptions cannot convey the flavor or the impact of a personal encounter with the charming Guru. Yet many people come to meet Baba Muktananda after reading those newspaper reports, for even those bare hints contain something of his essence. One woman read an article in the *San Francisco Examiner* which described Baba's stay in a San Francisco hospital and detailed the beneficial effects of his presence on the patients. She was so moved by the story that she began to cry and felt her heart filling with love. She called the newspaper to find out where she could meet Swami Muktananda, and later came to his Oakland Ashram. Another woman in Los Angeles said that she had heard an interview with him on the radio and that while listening to the program her mind had become calm and she had smelled a beautiful fragrance, which seemed to come from nowhere. She had received Shaktipat just by listening to Baba's voice.

Many of the reporters ask Muktananda the same basic questions: "What is a Guru?" "Why have you come to this country?" "What can meditation do for an ordinary person?"—the same questions that any person new to yoga would ask. Other reporters who are more familiar with the subject are able to go a little deeper with their questions, and understanding. It is Muktananda's way to always answer the person behind the question, rather than only the question itself. Often he gives different answers to the same questions, depending on the needs and understanding of the questioner. For this reason, none of these press interviews is ever routine, and some are filled with deep and subtle communication.

In Oakland, California, Muktananda devotees took over a derelict hotel and transformed it into a beautiful, residential Ashram in which Baba Muktananda lived for nearly a year, giving daily satsang *programs, and meditation Intensives on weekends. Local residents were delighted by the Ashram's influence on their neighborhood, as many devotees began to move into and refurbish houses throughout the surrounding area. During his Oakland stay, radio station KSAN of San Francisco recorded the following interview for a news program.*

KSAN: Would you describe Sidda Yoga?

Baba: Sidda Yoga is a very great yoga; it is the king of all yogas. You have to practice other yogas for a very long time, and even then a seeker rarely becomes centered in the superconscious, or final state of experience. But in Siddha Yoga, when you get the grace of a Siddha Guru who has received that grace from his Master, the inner divinity, or divine power—called Kundalini Shakti—is awakened. This is called Shaktipat initiation. Once this power is awakened through grace, it automatically takes you to higher and higher levels of experience until you reach a state of equanimity. After you receive this touch from a Master and the Shakti is awakened, everything happens automatically.

KSAN: Can you describe how you are able to transmit your energy to another person and how you choose who should receive it and who should not?

Baba: Generally speaking, from my own viewpoint and also from the viewpoint of the scriptures, all are equally fit to receive grace. There may be a few shortcomings in this or that person, but that doesn't matter. Such shortcomings can't prevent anyone from receiving grace. The Kundalini Shakti exists in good people as well as in the worst scoundrels; so we cannot say that because a person is wicked the Shakti is not there. Of course, some people may feel the awakening of the Shakti immediately and perceive such things as lights and visions. A few may suddenly soar to the highest level of experience. But for most, these experiences will come later.

KSAN: Do you have the power to awaken the Shakti in anybody you choose?

Baba: We conduct Intensives, or meditation courses, and you could say that those who attend have already been chosen in that only those who are ready to receive are present at these sessions. The awakening of the Shakti may not occur in perhaps four or five cases out of several hundred, but that doesn't matter. If those few people return again, they will surely get it. But instead of having just blind faith in what I am saying, it would be better for you to come and personally take part in one of the Intensives. Then you would have the experience directly.

KSAN: What is the most difficult problem your Western disciples have in following your teachings?

Baba: I don't find that these people have any difficulty at all in following my teachings. The only thing I really emphasize is that they should lead a clean life; they should be pure. I always emphasize this, and you will find this quality in all the members of our group. If they just hang around with me for a while—their addictions, such as smoking, drugs, and so on, seem to drop away automatically. Through this yoga they experience much more happiness and joy than they ever did before, so they don't need to seek pleasure through those things any more.

In the beginning they may find it difficult to sit calmly in one place for any length of time, but this becomes easy for them with a little practice. These people are very brave and have a lot of will-power. They can accomplish anything they set their hearts on.

KSAN: I know that a lot of Westerners who are trying to follow the spiritual path have trouble with the concept of reincarnation, and I'd like you to talk about this a bit.

Baba: It's true; Westerners do have difficulty with this concept. Still, reincarnation is a fact. Recently many people who did not previously believe in reincarnation have begun to recognize and accept its validity. When one's Shakti, one's hidden spiritual energy, is awakened through Siddha Yoga, one can directly perceive, in a vision, the realm of departed souls. Our scriptures declare that, once you have taken birth, you have to die, and once you die, you have to be born again. Because of this endless cycle of birth and death, the necessity for spirituality arose.

In India there are people who have detailed knowledge of their previous incarnations. Even so, I didn't attach much importance to this theory of reincarnation until, in the course of my meditations, I actually witnessed the existence of the departed souls in another realm. I was truly astonished.

KSAN: In what way do you feel your spiritual teachings can help the world? Or are you concerned only with individuals?

Baba: My teachings are helpful not only on an individual level, but also on a universal level. For instance, in America only one thing is lacking, and that is mental peace—a balanced state of mind. My yoga brings balance to the mind; it brings inner peace and steadiness, it gives strength and enthusiasm to do work, and it develops love and compassion toward other people. As an individual experiences more and more of his own Self, he naturally feels that all other souls, all other people, are part of his own being, and thus he develops more compassion and love for them. In the whole world, this alone can help other people—not political power or the power of money or the power of weapons. Only selfless love toward other people can be considered to be real wealth or accomplishment. You can see for yourself that we have grown to many thousands of people, and we all live together like one family. And in this family are all types of people: scientists, actors, engineers, astrologers, and there are people of every race, creed and nationality.

KSAN: Would you say something about your Guru and your lineage?

Baba: My Guru was a great ecstatic being. He was a born Siddha. Though he appeared to be simple, he was an omniscient being. He had gone beyond the mind. He would speak very little, remaining always in his own inner bliss. Whatever he spoke was the truth. If he gave you something in a loving way, you would get Shaktipat for sure, and if he took a stick and beat you or abused you, you would also get Shaktipat—he was such a great being. Even though he has left his body, he still meets me and gives me guidance, and he also appears to many of my followers in their meditations.

In a lineage that is authentic, the cosmic energy flows continuously from Master to disciple, generation after generation, from the very beginning of the tradition to the present time. Our lineage is called the Siddha tradition. There is a subtle realm of existence called Siddhaloka, and a great many enlightened beings—fully perfect Masters—live there. One who meditates can directly perceive this realm.

The Siddha lineage is a very ancient one, and it is fully charged with that cosmic energy. In our Intensives we explain all the details to those who attend, and then the Shakti, which is hidden inside everyone, is awakened. Once it is awakened, it never diminishes; it keeps growing.

KSAN: Do you need a Guru to awaken it?

Baba: To awaken the Shakti, it is absolutely essential to consult someone who is capable of awakening it within you. No matter what you want to accomplish in life, you first have to learn from someone who has already accomplished it. In the same way, to accomplish the awakening you must learn from an adept Master. Then, once the Shakti is awakened, the Shakti itself becomes the Master, guiding the student from within. Your own inner Shakti will direct you until you reach the state of perfection. At the end of your journey you will come to know that you are perfect and that you were always perfect.

For example, if you keep a wad of money in one of your pockets and you happen to search for that money in another pocket by mistake, you think, "Oh, I don't have any money! I'm broke!" If you tell a friend that you have lost your money and the friend points to the bulge in your other pocket, you immediately discover that you had the money all the time.

Just as you needed a friend to point out that your money was with you all along, so too the Guru is needed to point out to you the perfection that has been with you all along. The Guru awakens the Shakti; then the Shakti shows you your perfection.

KSAN: Perhaps you have some words of advice for someone who is seeking a Guru or seeking to be on the spiritual path.

Baba: People should have some basic understanding about Gurus. They should be able to tell whether a person who appears to be a Guru is really a Guru.

KSAN: How can you tell?

Baba: First, you have to find out whether this person who preaches about attaining great satisfaction and peace has attained these things himself. Then, after spending some time around a so-called Guru, if you don't notice any change or transformation in yourself, you should doubt that this person is the genuine article. If you approach a Guru, you should expect at least some positive change, and if there is no change taking place—if you continue to remain as you were before— what is the use in spending time with such a Guru?

To cure a disease we approach a doctor, but only after making all kinds of inquiries as to his capabilities and qualifications. Then, if he prescribes some pills for us, we have to find out whether they produce some positive results. We can't just keep swallowing everything he gives us even when we experience no benefit from it. It is a seeker's duty to test a prospective Guru very carefully.

Editor Joel Harris interviewed Baba Muktananda several times in Los Angeles. His magazine, The Movement, *is a spiritual community newspaper which features regular articles by Swami Muktananda.*

Joel Harris: What does your name mean, and how did you choose it?

Baba: A sannyasi, or an ordained monk, does not choose a name for himself; he does not have that right. A Guru gives him a name, depending on the sannyasi's worth and quality. The name Muktananda means *jivanmukta,* or one who has become liberated while still in the body. Only the name given to you by your Guru has value.

JH: What is your work on this planet?

Baba: To start a meditation revolution. I worked for it first in my own country, India, and now I have come to the West.

JH: What do you offer your disciples that they can't get anywhere else or from any other teacher?

Baba: You can give to devotees or disciples only what you yourself have; you can't give them what you don't have. If you went to a music teacher and expected him to teach you hatha yoga, would that be reasonable? I belong to the tradition of Siddha Yoga, and Siddha Yoga is not manifest in all teachers; it manifests in only a few.

JH: How does Siddha Yoga differ from other yogas?

Baba: Siddha Yoga encompasses all other forms of yoga because they become active in a Siddha student spontaneously. In every other form of yoga, you have to go to a Guru and learn techniques from him, whereas in Siddha Yoga all the yogic processes happen automatically once you receive the grace of a Siddha. That is why this yoga is considered to be superior to all other forms of yoga.

JH: Do you have a mantra that you use to communicate with God, and who gave you this mantra?

Baba: Mantra is the most important aspect of yoga. It removes the veil that exists between the individual and the spirit and makes them one. The mantra is always received from the Guru—one should never accept a mantra from an ordinary person. I received my mantra from my Guru, Nityananda, who was a great Siddha. That mantra was a gift of his grace. Through the mantra we enter our innermost consciousness.

JH: When and how did you come into this state of consciousness?

Baba: I attained this state through my Guru's grace and by following the path that he taught me. One gets into this consciousness the moment one is initiated by the Guru. I was initiated by my Guru in 1947. After that I carried on with the practices he had given me for about nine years until I reached the goal. Since then I have been in the same state.

JH: What basic delights do you enjoy in the physical world?

Baba: When you are in the liberated state, you are neither delighted nor repulsed by anything on the physical plane. However, what gives me great delight is to get people to meditate and chant and to help them move closer to God.

JH: You began your spiritual search when you were fifteen. Can you explain how it began?

Baba: The inspiration arose from inside. I was very fond of watching historical and religious plays, and around the age of eleven or twelve I also acted in them. I happened to see one very great play about two child devotees, Prahlada and Dhruva. The theme of the play was that these two children, though very young, meditated and practiced austerities and realized God, and that sank into my heart. Furthermore, my mother was a deeply religious woman, and right from my early childhood she had given me religious training. All of these factors combined to produce in me an intense longing to see the kingdom of God. So I left my home and wandered around India, and then, after a long, long time, I met my Guru, Swami Nityananda. He was a very great Siddha.

JH: What did your family say when you told them of your plan to find God?

Baba: When I left home I didn't tell anyone. I come from the south of India, and it was only after traveling thousands of miles and visiting the Himalayas that I wrote my family, telling them not to worry about me or to search for me.

JH: Were there any favorite places you used to visit when you were wandering?

Baba: I walked throughout the country on foot, and it takes a long time to completely walk around India. I was quite fond of Kashi (Benares) and the Himalayas. After I arrived in Maharashtra and settled there, I became quite fond of a sacred place called Pandharpur. Another place in Maharashtra that I am fond of is Alandi, which is where the samadhi shrine of Jnaneshwar is situated. I visit that place even now.

JH: Was there something you asked yourself or thought about when you were looking for God?

Baba: There was only one question in my mind, and that was: when shall I find my Guru, and when will he show God to me?

JH: Where did your wanderings lead you?

Baba: My wanderings eventually led me to Zipruanna, who was a great Siddha, a realized being. He directed me to my Guru. When I met my Guru my wanderings ended.

JH: Do you have any teachers now?

Baba: My Baba, Nityananda, was my final Guru. I don't need any other Guru now.

JH: Have you ever married?

Baba: Yes, I am married, but I am married to God. In India we get married only once; the question of getting married a second time could not arise.

JH: What do you think is the role of women in this age of enlightenment?

Baba: Women have a very significant role to play in the present age. Their role is as significant as that of men. You can't have man without woman, and you can't have woman without man. So, according to me, both have equal place. The body, whether it is that of a woman or a man, is a combination of equal parts of both parents, father and mother. In Indian culture women have a very high place. There is a Vedic mantra that says, "Honor your mother as God." The seers also enjoined us to honor our mothers as divine. Women enjoy great respect in India. They make distinguished contributions in all fields.

JH: An American proverb says, "Money is the root of all evil." What do you think of that?

Baba: Money is neutral. You can use it for good or evil ends; it depends on you. Whenever there are famines in other countries, Americans donate a lot of money, and that is a good use of wealth. Whether money will promote good or evil depends on the one who uses it.

JH: While traveling in the U.S., have you noticed a raising of consciousness among the young people in this country?

Baba: Yes, I see a great lift in the consciousness of young people here. They are spiritually awakened, and they are rising higher and higher.

JH: Is there anything that you have seen here which you would like to take back with you to India?

Baba: I find that Americans have beautiful hearts full of love, and I would like to take the American heart back with me.

JH: I don't know how you manage to stay so beautiful and young looking.

Baba: The secret is to live a life of discipline and to dwell constantly in the Self. I do not repeat the mantra of old age. I repeat only the mantra of youth and so, I remain young. I love only the Self, I find fulfillment only in the Self, and since I live my life and function in the Self, I remain young. I don't repeat the mantras that bring old age, such as anxiety and craving for sense pleasures. There is no youth like freedom from anxiety, and there is no old age like anxiety.

JH: My Self loves you. Thank you for your time.

Baba: I also thank you. You are full of love. You waited all morning for this interview, and you have asked your questions with great respect.

Sam Keen, an editor for the magazine Psychology Today, *met with Muktananda during his stay in Piedmont, California. Also present were others who had come to ask the Siddha Master various personal questions.*

Sam Keen: My heart has many scars and does not open easily. What should I do?

Baba: Are there really that many scars?

SK: It seems like many.

Baba: In spite of the scars, if you love your own inner Self, your heart will open automatically. If that doesn't work, try associating with a being whose heart is fully opened. If a person hangs out with one who smokes marijuana, he will learn to smoke it quite easily in only a few days. In the same way, if you hang out with one whose heart is fully open, you will be affected without much difficulty.

SK: I am troubled because most of the spiritual beings I have met seem to ignore the world. Their hearts may be open, but their eyes seem to be closed.

Baba: There are many whose eyes aren't closed to the world. If a Guru can turn a person who is weeping, wailing, and lamenting over his life in the world toward the peace and love dwelling within him, would you say his eyes are closed to the world? Thousands of people visit our Ashram in India. They include students, lawyers, military officers, politicians, and professionals. Those people whose inner hearts are opened, whose inner Shakti, or inner energy, is awakened through meditation, are able to function much better in the world. Students are able to perfect their studies, and professionals are able to perform their respective functions better.

SK: In the Indian tradition, turning inward was something that a person did after having fulfilled his family and social obligations. But here in America it seems that many young people are jumping ahead. They appear to be turning inward in order to avoid their outer obligations. What do you think about this?

Baba: If you really go within through meditation, then, by the help of what you find there, you will function very efficiently and effectively in your outer life. In our present condition we have only limited power. But if we turned within, we would get in touch with the source of infinite energy, and by tapping that energy we could improve our lives.

SK: How can one love wisdom if he has not first tasted folly?

Baba: If you can taste wisdom without tasting folly, what's the point of tasting folly? There was a great king in India who was very highly evolved; his name was Bhartrihari. In a Sanskrit verse he says, "As long as your body is strong, as long as your senses are strong, as long as you have many, many years to live, you should turn within and discover the Shakti, or energy, which exists there and use it in your outer life."

In ancient India, because people had learned to turn within, they could live their lives in the world very beautifully. They performed their duties in the world and enjoyed their family life; yet at the same time they remained in contact with their inner reality. So they were quite at peace with themselves and with the world outside.

It is only before true understanding dawns that you find the world to be an obstacle. After you have attained true understanding of things, the world is a source of great joy. There was a time when I used to wander from forest to forest, seeking solitude. But now I don't seek solitude; I enjoy it in the midst of the world.

Infinite Shakti, which is also infinite bliss, lives within us. Whatever happiness we experience through outer pleasures passes like a flash of lightning because that happiness is merely a reflection of the inner bliss. The happiness I feel does not come from any of the outer activities. For example, suppose your wife or husband is looking at you with love. The intellect becomes still, and then happiness bubbles up from inside. Instead of recognizing that the source of that happiness is within us, we project that happiness onto the other person and think that it is coming from him. One should seek the source of happiness again and again because it is divine in its nature. That source of happiness is the ultimate truth, and it is also the final realization. It is the inner Self. Therefore, it is necessary that everyone remember the inner Self all the time. This the highest religion for man.

The interviewers from Laughing Man Magazine *were informed seekers who had read Muktananda's spiritual autobiography,* Play of Consciousness, *and wished to ask him questions concerning his initiation by Swami Nityananda.*

LM: Our next issue will be about the eye and perception. The first question we'd like to ask has to do with *drishti diksha,* initiation by look. In your book, *Play of Consciousness,* you describe how you received initiation through Bhagawan Nityananda's look—the *Parashiva shambhavi mudra.* Could you explain that?

Baba: There are four ways in which Siddhas initiate. One is *drishti diksha,* by their look, through which they transmit the inner Shakti to the initiate. This is also called *mayura diksha,* or initiation in the manner of a peacock. It is said that, when mating, the male peacock doesn't touch the female peacock; he impregnates her just by a look. The second is initiation through touch, or *sparsha diksha.* The touch can be in any form; a Siddha can physically touch you, he can throw an object at you, or he can grab you between the eyebrows, where the *ajna chakra* is situated. This method of initiation by touch is the specialty of the Siddhas, and they do it any way they like. The third way is initiation through thought. They just think about it, and the person gets initiated. This is also called initiation by grace, or *kripa.* The fourth initiation is through word, or *shabda diksha.* In this method, some mantra or sound is whispered into the ear of the disciple. These are the four varieties of initiation.

LM: We are particularly interested in learning about initiation through the eye.

Baba: One who gives this *drishti diksha,* or initiation through look, should be an *urdhva drishta,* one who has the upward-turned look; one whose gaze is downwardly inclined cannot give such an initiation. Perception, or vision, is of two varieties: one is downward and outward in direction, and the other is upward and inward. If you look at the pictures of great saints such as Nityananda Baba and Shirdi Sai Baba, you will see that their eyes are looking upward. Their way of looking is always with this upward focus, never downward; even when they appear to look down, their eyes will always maintain that upward-looking quality. That look is very significant. Even though the eyes are open and appear to be looking outside, actually, the attention is fixed within their own being. They are perceiving their own Self within.

Real Gurus have the power to initiate a person by all four means. They initiate some through look, some through word, some through touch, and some through thought. All four means of initiation are equally effective; all four take the disciple to the ultimate point of knowledge, that is, an actual experience of knowledge, not knowledge based on mere intellectual understanding.

LM: Would you tell us, Baba, a little about your initiation by Swami Nityananda, whose gaze, it is said, would dispel all karma and suffering?

Baba: I was with him for a long time before I received initiation. On that day—August 15, 1947—when I went for his *darshan,* he looked a little different than usual. He was wearing a beautiful pair of wooden sandals, and he was walking back and forth, smiling. He came near me and smiled and began to sing. Then he gazed directly at me, his eyes merging with mine. I couldn't feel my body. The divine splendor of his eyes completely stilled my own eyes. I had no power to open or close them. We remained like this for a while. Then Gurudev stepped back and uttered his characteristic ''hunh'' sound. I partially regained consciousness. Then he offered me the sandals he was wearing and told me to put them on. I was amazed, but replied reverently and firmly, ''Gurudev, these sandals are not to be worn by me. They are for me to worship all my life. Please be so gracious as to leave them in my shawl.''

Gurudev agreed. Making the same humming sounds, he lifted one foot at a time and placed the sandals in the shawl. He stood directly in front of me and looked into my eyes once more. I watched him very attentively. A ray of light was coming from his pupils and going right inside me. Its touch was searing, red, and hot; its brilliance dazzled my eyes like a high-powered blub. As this ray of light flowed from his eyes into mine, the hair on my body rose with wonder, awe, ecstasy, and fear. I repeated the mantra *Guru Om* as I watched this unbroken stream of divine radiance. Sometimes it was the color of molten gold, sometimes saffron, and sometimes a deep blue. I stood there stunned, watching the brilliant rays passing into me. My body was completely motionless. Then Baba moved and again made his "hunh" sound. I became conscious and found that I could move a little.

Some days after that he told me to pursue my *sadhana* at a place about one hundred fifty miles from Ganeshpuri. I lived in a hut in the country, and I began to practice meditation under a mango tree. It was there that I began to experience the unfoldment of the divine Shakti. It was amazing.

LM: What happened?

Baba: During that time, many things happened; generally, we don't reveal all these experiences. It was about nine-thirty in the evening and I was meditating. Suddenly my legs locked into the lotus posture, and my tongue curled up into my nasal passage. I looked around me, and the whole sugar cane field nearby was on fire. I saw fire everywhere. I tried to get up and run away, but I couldn't because my legs were locked in the lotus position. I saw this great conflagration all around me, and all I could hear was the sound of the bursting and crackling of sugar cane. It was such a terrifying experience that I almost lost consciousness. Then my head went forward and touched the ground, and I became completely unconscious. I don't know how long I was in that position. When I finally woke up, I raised my head and saw that it was sunrise, and I heard the sound of the birds. Automatically, my legs unlocked. My whole body was aching. I thought that my mind was not steady because all night long I had been having visions of many, many things. But then I went into the sugar cane field and saw that the field was completely intact. I thought my mind was completely deluded, and I became very unhappy. I was so restless that something had gone wrong with my *sadhana* and that perhaps my mind had become unbalanced.

It was then that a saint named Harigiri Baba, whom I knew very well, came to visit me in a *tonga,* a horse-drawn cart. He said, "Don't be scared, Muktananda, and don't worry. Your fever is a very beneficial one." (He had his own peculiar language.) Then he demanded two rupees to pay for the cart, took the money, and went away.

I left my hut the same day and walked quite some distance into the forest. I came to a farm and was met by a farmer, a nice man who also practiced yoga. He asked me to stay there, and in his house I saw a book about Siddha Yoga. I opened the book at random and read a page. I was astonished to find the details of what had happened to me the previous day. Then I became very happy. I remained there and continued my *sadhana* for quite some time, having many experiences. It would take a very long time to narrate all those experiences here, but they are described completely in *Play of Consciousness*. I did not have just a couple of experiences, such as the experience of formlessness and namelessness. Such experiences are only the beginning. These beginning experiences become meaningless compared to the countless higher experiences that come later. It was after the initial effects of Shaktipat that my real yoga started, and this yoga was spontaneous. I saw each and every *nadi* in the body—all seventy-two thousand of the subtle channels through which the life-force, or prana, flows. I experienced the direct perception of the movement or play of consciousness within all these *nadis*. I also came to understand the nature of the heart and saw how the mind wanders from point to point in the heart. I saw that the heart center and the thousand-petaled spiritual center, in the crown of the head, are not at all different; they are made of the same stuff. The individual soul does not reside only in the heart but also in the thousand-petaled lotus. If the individual soul resided only in the heart, a person would live even if you cut off his head. But such a thing doesn't happen, because the soul also resides in the head.

LM: Swami, your own gaze is very powerful, and it occasions all kinds of emotions and experiences in many people who are strangers to yoga. Perhaps you could tell us a little about what happens to you when you look at them.

Baba: When I look at others, I see them as my own Self. If the Lord were to appear here in person, He wouldn't look at you as a reporter and me as a Swami; He would see both of us as exactly the same. Even if He tried, He couldn't see differences. Therefore, only when a Guru looks at someone and sees his own Self can Shaktipat by glance take place. Similarly, if you look at someone for whom you have great feeling, the love automatically flows into that person.

LM: You speak of a certain point in your own *sadhana* when there was a piercing of your own physical eye by the Shakti, by Consciousness. Could you speak about the change in the eye itself as a result of this awakening?

Baba: The normal eyes of a human being generally see diversity in objects and people. In the course of *sadhana*, a process called *bindu bheda* takes place; it is a very painful process in which the eyes begin to revolve very fast. Then the eyes get the power to see within. One's entire power of perception completely changes; you look at people with a positive attitude all the time.

After *bindu bheda,* you see the Blue Pearl. It comes out of the eye and stands before you. But even that is not the culmination of *sadhana;* there is something beyond the experience which cannot be described. Only after the vision of the Blue Pearl does one experience that indescribable state. Only then does one develop true witness-consciousness all the time. Witness-consciousness means that you see yourself in the same way as you see other things or people. Even while performing all your activities, you continuously remain in witness-consciousness.

To describe this state as being beyond all description is not to describe it adequately. Even a drug addict or a drunkard gets into that kind of transcendental state for a while. But to get such an experience with complete awareness makes all the difference. When a person gets established in that state with awareness, he never again becomes a slave to the senses; all the senses become his slaves. One who is established in the Self is completely independent, because the Self is completely free.

If your mind constantly runs after this or that, wanting this or desiring that, and at the same time you say that your mind is in a transcendental state, you are just talking childish nonsense; you are playing make-believe. One should acquire complete independence— so much so that in his company other people also have a similar experience of independence.

LM: Thank you very much, Swami. We certainly appreciate the time you have given us.

Baba: We shall meet again. If a person contemplates these ideas, he can reach a very, very high state.

Donovan Bess was a reporter for the San Francisco Chronicle *until he met Baba in Piedmont and quit his job to join the Muktananda entourage. During Baba's visit to Oklahoma City, Bess arranged for him to be interviewed by* Oklahoma City Times' *Wain Miller, who came to the house where Muktananda was staying. While introducing Miller to the Swami, Bess presented his Guru with a personal gift of a woolen scarf, which Baba spontaneously wrapped around the neck of the new reporter. This gesture prompted the reporter's first question.*

Wain Miller: Are you trying to bribe me?

Baba: Why should I bribe you? What can you do for me? If you could plead my case with God, that would be fine; but of what use is anything else to me?

WM: Do you have many problems with skeptics?

Baba: All kinds of people come to me, including skeptics. A holy man is just like the banks of a river to which all kinds of people come.

WM: Do you retaliate against people who put you down?

Baba: For what? Why should I bother? The fact is that if you insult somebody or are unkind to somebody, you are really insulting yourself. The same Consciousness fills everyone; so whatever you do, whether good or bad, you do to yourself, not to somebody else. For example, if I think ill of you, I am the first one to suffer from those negative thoughts in my heart. They might affect you later, but first it is my mind which is polluted.

WM: Is it true that man accumulates merit in this birth by which he goes to either heaven or hell?

Baba: Yes, reincarnation is a reality. There are many saints in India who, during meditation, have visited *Pitruloka,* the world of ancestors. After you get into deep meditation, if your awareness focuses on the heart, you are able to see seven of your past lives. Moreover, you can also see whether you are going to be reborn.

WM: Can you report on what you saw of your past lives?

Baba: In one life I was the king of a small state; in another I was a warrior. In a couple of lives, I saw myself practicing yoga and meditation intensely.

WM: Will you be born again, and, if so, when and in what form?

Baba: Why should I be born again? You are reborn only for the fulfullment of desires that you still have. My only interest is God and the highest truth, and so I don't think I will fall into the cycle of birth and death again. However, I am totally at His disposal; if He wanted me to come back again at some time to do the kind of work I am doing now, I would have no objection.

WM: Does one decide oneself whether to continue to live in the world serving man or to merge into the true reality?

Baba: If your destiny is to work in the world, even if you have merged into the supreme Consciousness, you continue to work in the world totally merged with the highest state of consciousness as long as you are required to. But such a being is no longer tormented by desire or pleasure and pain as he was earlier.

WM: Does a being who has merged into the Absolute, but remains to teach others, suffer physical ailments?

Baba: The body is subject to natural laws. Physical ailments—such as those caused by change of climate—may arise because the body is subject to all those things. If you drive a car constantly, then, at times, something may go wrong with it. But if something goes wrong with the car, it doesn't mean that something has gone wrong with the person sitting in the car.

The Pacifica Radio Network's representative had already attended several Intensives and retreats with Muktananda before coming to interview him at the DeVille Hotel, his temporary Ashram in New York's Catskill Mountains. This taped interview was for a program to be broadcast by many of the network's associate radio stations throughout the country.

PRN: What is a Siddha Guru?

Baba: One who is perfect in everything is called a Siddha Guru. A being who has attained independence from his inner senses as well as his outer senses is called a Siddha Guru. Usually man is dependent on sensual gratification. He is dependent on touch, taste, words or sounds, and form. He is also under the control of the six enemies: lust, anger, infatuation, greed, pride, and jealousy. He becomes a puppet and dances according to the mind's command. But a Siddha has learned to control all these things—the six enemies, all the senses, and the mind. He can do anything with them, and that's why he's called a Siddha, a perfected being. A Siddha Guru is completely independent; he has realized God. He holds or stores God's Shakti inside himself and is able to make other people realize this Shakti inside themselves. A Siddha is one who is not attracted by anything but to whom everything is attracted.

PRN: Spokesmen for different paths often claim that it is not necessary to have a Guru in order to achieve the state of total realization. Do you agree?

Baba: An individual might say this, but, so far, no representative of a respectable tradition has ever said this. None of the great beings, such as Lord Buddha, Shankaracharya, and Guru Nanak, have ever said that you don't need a Guru. If you don't need a Guru, you don't need a doctor, either. You don't need an engineer, an architect, or a governor to rule the state. Likewise, you don't need a mate for your family life, and you don't need a friend either. But if you need all these, then the Guru is absolutely necessary too; you need him very badly. Do the paths that say you don't need a Guru also say you don't need a mate, a doctor, an engineer, and all the others? Do they say that you don't have to eat or drink? They don't say this, do they? Why do they say you don't need a Guru? All this means is that they don't have any understanding about a Guru.

PRN: Is there a danger of becoming too dependent on the safety and regularity of being with the Guru in the ashram environment and not being able to maintain a state of love and bliss in the marketplace?

Baba: You don't see any danger when you become dependent on a wife, so why should you think about this danger when you become dependent on a Guru? Why do you think that when you are with a Guru it will be dangerous? A Guru also lives among people. The Oakland Ashram is surrounded by nightclubs and bars, but none of my people have been spoiled. Living with a Guru will not spoil you. On the contrary, those people who are corrupt and spoiled can be reformed by being with a Guru. Many boys and girls who were mentally agitated came to live with me for a while, and they became well. Many people in the world don't know how to lead their lives. They have to consult a psychic or a psychologist; so they are depending on these people while living in the world. By living in the Ashram you become very independent and courageous. After you attain Shakti, after you become the embodiment of Shakti, you don't become dull or dependent; you become very active and intelligent, and you can do your work better.

PRN: If the purpose of the Guru is to make his disciples like himself how many of your disciples have become totally realized, like you?

Baba: I haven't yet counted the number of realized beings among my people. But if they have received Shaktipat, that is more than enough, because this Shakti will take them to the final state—it will make them realized beings. The Shakti that you receive continues to increase inside you, and it doesn't matter what work you are doing. The Shakti will work inside you for a long time, and eventually you will perceive the truth. In America, many, many people have received Shakti from me; so there must be some people who have become realized. But I don't keep a count.

PRN: Does everyone who is touched by you eventually become your disciple?

Baba: Yes, to receive Shakti is to become a disciple.

PRN: Does a Guru's effectiveness diminish when he has a large number of disciples?

Baba: A Guru should be perfect; he should not be even a little bit imperfect. A great Guru is absolutely perfect, and his power won't diminish if the number of disciples increases. Sometimes a Guru has to suffer the various karmas of his disciples; so at those times he becomes sick.

Now, if I give Shakti to a person, that Shakti is not necessarily going to catch him immediately. Only when his merits and demerits become balanced will the Shakti catch him and will he begin to experience it. When a Guru gives his Shakti to a disciple, the karmas from that disciple's countless lives go to the Guru in the form of diseases, and that's why all the great beings become sick at some time or another; but it doesn't matter, because the sickness doesn't affect them—only their bodies are affected. A Guru is not the body; he is the Shakti, the energy. He is the grace-bestowing power of God. The Shakti is never afflicted by diseases, and the Self never contracts them either. It is because of destiny that the Guru contracts the diseases of his disciples, but after a while he becomes free of those diseases.

PRN: Do you feel that the Indian rituals and practices that you have brought here are essential in order for people to experience who they really are and become totally realized?

Baba: The main purpose of these rituals of worship is to purify the atmosphere. The performance of these rituals helps to maintain the purity of a place so that it is easy to feel Shakti there. It's only because you don't know the Indian language that you consider these rituals as part of the Hindu religion. If you understood the meaning of the chants, you would begin to feel that they were yours. I will explain this very briefly. For example, every evening we sing the *Arati* in praise of the Guru because we don't consider the Guru to be merely a human being; we consider him to be God. The *Arati* says, "O supreme Guru, kindle my light with your light. Inside me lies the dormant Kundalini Shakti; awaken this Kundalini with your light." Is there anything specifically Indian in this? Only the language belongs to India. But the real meaning, the essence, is not Indian, nor does it belong to any other country.

If someone sang this in English, should I then say that it belongs only to the Christian tradition? It's man's imagination that creates these different religious castes. These castes are confined only to human beings; they cannot reach God—they cannot even go to the door of God. Only when man goes beyond all religions can he find room in God's house. Only because you don't understand the meaning behind the language are you confused. The *Gita* says, "Abandon all religions, and take refuge in the inner Self, in the inner truth." I haven't brought anything new to America; whatever I've brought is already here. Kundalini Shakti is already within you. If I awaken your Kundalini, I awaken your own Kundalini; I don't put mine inside you. So what have I brought from India?

PRN: Do you have any message for the American people?

Baba: The first part of my message to the people of America is: "God is within you and He is fully conscious. Perceive Him, listen to Him, and meditate on Him." The second part of my message is: "Just as He is within you, He is within everyone. Therefore, you should respect others and treat them as your true friends." The third part of my message is: "Everyone is the child of God; that is why you should have compassion toward other people. Perform good actions. It is you who will have to bear all your karmas, just as you have to eat the fruit of what you have sown in the earth; and that is why you should perform only good actions."

There are a great number of mentally ill people in America. You should think about this and try to find out why. There is not as much of this sickness in other countries and the reason for this should be discovered.

A doctor who works in a mental hospital in New York came to meet me and asked if he could bring a busload of boys and girls. It seems that, when some of our people recently visited the hospital and began to chant, those children became affected. They began to chant too, and became very absorbed. In fact, all of the patients became interested, and so the doctor wanted to bring them to the Ashram. I asked him how many cases of disturbed children were there, and he replied, "Three thousand." When I heard that, I just couldn't speak; I couldn't say anything.

The people of America should try to find out why this sickness is increasing. You have reached Mars, and you are going to Venus, but you have left the Earth without discovering anything about it. People don't know how to conceive a child; that's why this illness is happening. First, they take psychedelic drugs or drink a lot, and then they conceive their children. In America people take so many drugs, pills, and other things, and all these affect the child; these things permeate the fetus and have their corresponding influence on the child.

What is the use of a nation whose children are ill? What can such a nation achieve?

So my final message for everyone is: "Meditate on your Self, worship your Self, kneel to your Self, understand your Self; your God dwells within you as you." If you want to see God, you don't have to pursue God or follow any religion; just shower your compassion on people without any expectation, and then God will reveal Himself to you.

2
SPIRITUALITY
IN THE WORLD

For many of the people who come to meet Swami Muktananda, the idea of a Guru is unfamiliar and rather frightening. The relationship between a Guru and his disciples is a difficult one for Westerners to understand, and it is often viewed with cynicism. The Western concept of personal freedom does not easily incorporate the idea that submission to a true spiritual authority can be a help rather than a hindrance to personal development. When people express their fears to Muktananda about getting involved with a Guru, he often points out to them the inconsistencies in their attitudes. He explains: "People don't hesitate to accept the help of teachers in order to learn an art or skill, they don't hesitate to consult a doctor for medical advice, nor do they mind relying on experts in every other field. Then why does the Guru stick in their throats?"

Many of the Americans who come to see Baba Muktananda are not directly looking for a spiritual guide. They are well educated and successful and their lives, on the surface, seem to lack nothing. Yet they suffer from persistant feelings of discontent. They suspect that there is something more to life, some satisfaction beyond the pleasures of career and personal relationships, but they aren't sure just what it is. As a prominent California psychologist put it to Baba, "I have received the best education available, have hundreds of students, and have no particular problems, but I don't feel any love or inner strength." A lawyer from New York described it this way: "Although I had personal happiness and material wealth, I still felt empty inside. Meditation has made me full; now my life is more joyous and fulfilled."

These people who come to Muktananda seeking something they don't quite understand, are in no way unique. The cultural patterns in America over the past thirty years have reflected an increasingly widespread and urgent desire for greater self knowledge. People have been looking for themselves everywhere: through psychoanalysis and psychotherapy, through drugs, through encounter groups and human potential movements, and through Eastern philosophies and practices. Even though Americans are reluctant to call themselves seekers, it is clear that many are looking for something that they cannot find outside of themselves. It is often said that when the disciple is ready the Guru appears. It is the desire for knowledge on the part of the seeker which attracts the Guru. Thus, hundreds of spiritual teachers and masters have come to America.

Many teachers can talk convincingly about the existence of our inner divinity. But the real test of a Guru is whether he can make you experience that divinity within yourself. This is the quality that sets Baba Muktananda apart from other teachers. He has given that experience of inner awakening to thousands of Americans. He has fully realized his own spiritual perfection, and he also sees everyone else as perfect, pure, and radiant, bound only by their own limited images of themselves. Muktananda works to eradicate his disciples' sense of smallness and makes them aware of their own divinity. He will never accept that man is a sinner. Not only does he tell people they are perfect, he gives them the experience of their own perfection.

The problem, though, for most people is how to pursue their inner Self. "I can't go running off to the Himalayas to live in a cave," people complain. "How am I to proceed?" Muktananda gives a very simple answer. "Meditate. In the midst of your normal life, just find a little time for meditation. Meditation will give you renewed energy and competence for work. Meditation will release your inner joy and love and increase your enjoyment of family and friends. Meditation will sharpen your mind and intellect and enhance your powers of concentration.''

At first people find it difficult to believe that by taking a few minutes for themselves each day to meditate their lives will be altered. For a beginner, daily sessions of meditation may seem tedious, but once a meditator has received the subtle energy of the Guru, he finds that meditation becomes easy and spontaneous; the effort is taken out of it. And for those who have received Shaktipat and who are under Muktananda's guidance, the gross and subtle life-transformations are breathtaking. As one man described his experience during an Intensive: ''At the first Intensive I didn't have any experiences in meditation, but a seed started to grow inside of me and I had a lot of faith in Baba. I introduced him to my family, and now one day a week we all sit together for meditation. My children used to fight a lot, but they have completely changed. To this day I still have not had any experiences in meditation, but my family has been completely transformed and become more loving. Now I understand that you shouldn't expect a certain kind of experience, but just to get what he wants to give you.''

To Muktananda there is no separation between spiritual and mundane life. He sees without the usual preconceptions that divide the mind from the body, and the body from the spirit. Thus, he is able to diagnose the source of a seeker's dissatisfaction and can determine immediately whether a ''spiritual'' or a ''practical'' prescription is required. There is a story about how he once sent one of his disciples away from the Ashram in Ganeshpuri telling him to go and drive a cab in New York City: ''For you, right now, money is more important than God.'' The disciple did what his Guru instructed him to do, and while he was driving his taxi, he had as many ''spiritual'' experiences as he had had during his time in Muktananda's Ashram in India. Muktananda has always said that many of the greatest saints realized their inner Self not by leaving the world, but by embracing it. But it is only when we have the understanding given by a Guru that the world becomes a true school for Self-knowledge. Without this understanding we are buffeted about, without anchor, in the rounds of pleasure and pain which daily life provides for us.

This chapter includes a selection of short talks given by Swami Muktananda on the need for meditation in daily life and the need for persistence and one-pointedness in spiritual practice. Also included are answers to questions from seekers on the relationship between everyday life and spiritual techniques.

HAPPINESS LIES WITHIN

"Man has a yearning for all kinds of pleasures in his life so he looks to sense objects for happiness. He wants to get high and swim in bliss all the time so he takes up many different activities. But instead of finding happiness, he finds only misery; instead of finding ecstasy, he finds only dejection.

"I once read a story by Ram Tirth. A man built a temple of mirrors, and in the middle of the temple he put a big rose with open petals. All its beauty was revealed. He also put a pigeon inside the temple. When the pigeon saw all the reflections of the rose in the mirrors, he began to fly from one to another, hoping to get a taste of the rose. He kept pecking at all those mirrors until he became exhausted and fell down. He landed on the rose, and finally he was happy. That is the predicament we are in. Though happiness is very close to us— inside our own being—we keep looking for it outside, in all kinds of reflections and temptations.

"Life can be lived with great joy and happiness if we turn within and meditate. At present, our lives are without real joy, without real sweetness, because we put our trust in outer things. We fail to understand that if our inner Shakti were awakened, we would find everything inside us. Inner growth, inner awakening, inner evolution, and inner meditation give an immediate pay-off. In the beginning, we may not enjoy turning within that much, because we are not acquainted with our inner world. But there is great bliss there. When we get to know the inner world, we also get to know the outer world, and then we become aware that the outer world is not just an artistic creation, but a sport, an expansion of Consciousness. It's a wonder that man journeys with such great enthusiasm to so many external places, no matter how distant they are, but he doesn't like to visit that place inside him, which is very close. A poet says, "Your weeping will not cease, nor can you admire the strength of the spirit, unless you turn within."

"In our spare time, right in the midst of our worldly life, we can get something very great by turning within—we can attain divinity— because within us is the same divine power that created the universe.

"Therefore, let meditation enter your daily life and permeate your daily activities. No matter what you do, what you eat or drink, what you give or take, you should learn to see Consciousness in all these things. Meditation doesn't mean just sitting in a solitary place for a short while. Even when we make sandwiches, we should be able to see

Consciousness in that, too. If we become aware of Consciousness in our every single activity, meditation becomes easy. Once we forget Consciousness, we forget ourselves, and then we also forget God. It is Consciousness which has become everything and is present everywhere.

"The Upanishads say there is nothing but Consciousness outside, and there is nothing but Consciousness inside; nothing is different from Consciousness. Whatever you see is just another form of Consciousness. With this knowledge, you will not forget your Self nor will you let others forget the Self in them. This knowledge is true knowledge, and it is the greatest kind of meditation.

"Don't live in the hope that you will attain happiness from the external world. Everything you seek is within you. If you want to become very happy, then go within, because happiness lies within you. And if you are seeking love, then seek it within, because love also lies within you. God has stored everything inside you. Don't seek anything outside. Give up all hope of ever finding anything outside. Always worship your Self and think of your Self as pure Consciousness, as God. Become happy all the time within your Self, and think of your Self as very great. There is no greatness beyond the Self, there is no love beyond the Self, and there is no pleasure beyond the Self. My blessings today are with the hope that you will always reside within the Self."

SADHANA

"Man should constantly pursue his *sadhana,* or spiritual practice. Just as we don't decide to give up eating food simply because we happen to have eaten a great meal, likewise, we shouldn't give up our *sadhana* simply because we have received a few spiritual experiences. *Sadhana* should not stop until we attain the state of perfection.

"There once was a king called Shivaji, who kept a careful watch over the activities of his subjects. One night, as he was making his rounds of the city, he observed a man filtering sand by the light of a small lamp. The king sat on his horse in front of the man, who was so engrossed in his task that he didn't even notice the king. The king watched for some time as the man sifted sand, searching for tiny particles of gold. Then, before leaving, the monarch removed his golden armlet, which was studded with diamonds, and dropped the precious ornament into the sand the man was sifting.

"In those days, there were certain kings who were very kind and sincerely interested in the well-being of their subjects. They did not spend their time just enjoying all the royal comforts and pleasures. In India the kings were considered to be gods; they were not tyrants who would take all the people's money for their own enjoyment.

"The next night, when the king visited that place again, he observed the man still filtering sand by the light of a small lamp. After some time, the king finally got the man's attention by saying, 'Listen, why are you still filtering sand? Didn't you find anything last night?'

"The man nodded, 'Yes, I did find something very valuable.'

'That ornament was worth enough to take care of you for your entire life,' the king remarked. 'Why are you doing the same work again tonight?'

"The man replied, 'I got something so valuable just by sifting sand for a few days. Who knows what treasure could be mine if I do this for an entire lifetime?'

"In the same way, we should not stop our spiritual practice just because we have a few experiences now and then. We should not be satisfied with just a little; we have to continue our *sadhana* until we attain perfection. Some people, as soon as they have some small experiences, like a few *kriyas* or a vision of lights, immediately think that their work is over and that they can become gurus, and they start collecting their own disciples.

"I once read a story about a great mendicant. In olden days, mendicants practiced the art of alchemy, a secret art by which base metal is converted into gold with the help of special herbs.

"One day two seekers approached this alchemist and asked to become apprentices. The master agreed, and for some time the pair lived with the alchemist, trying to learn the secret of turning base metal into gold. But masters won't generally impart the highest knowledge without first carefully observing the quality of the disciple. They usually keep the disciple with them for quite some time, and only then do they impart the highest secret.

"One day both of the disciples were frying some beans on a metal plate, and they were stirring the beans with a stick. Though they didn't know it, the stick was made of the secret herbal mixture, and as they were stirring the beans, the plate began turning yellow and soon became gold. When they saw the plate turn into gold, they thought they had attained perfection in alchemy. They threw away the stick, grabbed the golden plate, and ran away.

"This is what happens in our spiritual practice also. People come to the Intensives and as soon as they receive the touch on the first day, think, "Well, I've got it. There's nothing more to get here." and they go to the registration counter and ask for a refund for the second half of the Intensive! Even in their spiritual practice, some people are corrupt.

"Our goal is a very lofty one: to reach the state of divinity itself—nothing less. For that, we have to pursue continuous *sadhana*. We have to renew our commitment to it again and again."

ONE-POINTEDNESS

"The Bhagavad Gita states that he who does not have one-pointedness—complete faith in just one thing—will always be going in several different directions at the same time, never getting far in any of them. Just as one cannot hope to cross the sea with each foot in a different boat, neither can you attain the goal of spirituality unless you have one-pointed devotion and one-pointed faith.

"Someone asked the great saint Tulsidas, 'How is your sadhana going?'

"Tulsidas replied, 'My *sadhana* is to believe in God, to have faith in God, to repeat the mantra of God, to see God, and to live in God. That's all I know about it.'

"We should all practice this kind of one-pointedness, but, unfortunately, most of us do not. Kabir, who was also a very great saint, said that most people have only a little faith but a lot of doubts. When doubt overcomes faith, we become like the washerman's dog.

"In India the washermen launder clothing on the river banks, and each one always has a donkey to carry the laundry from his house to the river. He also has a dog with him to watch over the clothing after it is washed and set out to dry, while the washerman has a nap.

"One day, while a washerman was washing clothes, his dog got hungry and, fearing that its master was so busy he would forget to feed it, ran home for its food. But the people at home thought that the dog had already been fed at the river; so they didn't offer it anything. When it saw that it wasn't going to get fed at the house, it ran back to the river bank where, by that time, the washerman was just finishing his lunch. Seeing the dog come from the direction of his house, the washerman assumed that the dog had been fed at home and the dog missed out on this meal too, simply because it lacked complete faith in its master. The donkey, however, never doubted that it would be taken care of. It remained at the river with one-pointed devotion and got its lunch.

FAITH

"Likewise, man should be one-pointed in doing his *sadhana*. It is faith which uplifts you and the lack of faith which pulls you down. I just remembered another story, which I read long ago.

"There were two friends who were great thieves, and they knew that skill very well. As they were both getting on in years, they decided to give up their lives of crime and do something good for a change. So they both approached a very famous saint, confessed all their sins, and requested the saint's blessing along with a mantra.

"It is a custom in India for Gurus to always impart mantras in secret, either in writing, as we do with mantra cards, or by whispering the mantra into the seeker's ear. The saint called the thieves to him, one at a time, and said, 'I am going to impart a divine mantra. If you constantly repeat it and never reveal it to another person, you will surely end up in heaven.' Then he whispered a mantra to each of them.

"The thieves were very happy, and they both repeated their secret mantras for several years with one-pointed faith. One day, they both died—at the very same time—and, sure enough, a plane came down from heaven and took both of them aboard. (You see, it is through faith and devotion that a mantra bears fruit, not just mere repetition of words. When you repeat *Om Namah Shivaya*, it is not only those words which are very powerful, but also your faith in that mantra which is very powerful; it is that faith which will liberate you.)

"As the two thieves sat inside the vehicle from heaven, flying higher and higher, they were so happy that they embraced each other and began to talk excitedly about how they had once stolen and repented together, had done *sadhana* together, and now had become liberated together, 'What great mantras we both received,' one exclaimed. 'Mine was so simple; yet it bore such wonderful fruit.'

'Mine was simple too,' the other said, 'I just repeated *da da da da*.'

'And I repeated *ku ku ku ku*,' confided his friend.

"As soon as they put the two mantras together, they realized that that the saint had given them the mantra *daku,* which means "thief" in Hindi. Both men became furious. 'What a scoundrel that saint was!' they exclaimed. 'He fooled us!' The moment they said this, the plane turned upside down.

"So it is faith which uplifts you, and it is doubt which makes you fall. We should have supreme faith in our *sadhana,* in all our spiritual practices, and in our mantra. Only then can we really achieve something inside. Only because we lack faith do we feel that we haven't attained what is already attained, for, truly speaking, supreme bliss is always with us."

Q. Aren't yoga and meditation either for the idle, who have a lot of time on their hands, or for the poor, distressed, and downtrodden, who have misery in their lives? Where does the middle class fit in?

Baba: What makes you think that the only things the middle class should pursue are eating, drinking, watching TV, visiting clubs and discos, and seeing movies? What kind of teaching is it that says yoga and meditation are not meant for the middle class? I refuse to believe that all one's time must be spent in earning a living; there must be some free time. Meditation has nothing to do with poverty or wealth. Meditation is meant for people who are intelligent and conscious— people who have human dignity and discrimination. Only people who are stupid and unconscious are not aware of what it means to be human. Such people remain caught up all the time in working for a living; they are not any different from animals, beasts of burden, or machines.

Man is not meant to live the life of a machine, an ox, a bull, or a donkey; he was created to live a different kind of life. In no field of work are you required to work for twenty-four hours every day. No matter how hard you work, you have time for meditation, provided that you have an urge to meditate. One gets so much energy from meditation that one would be able to work for sixteen hours, instead of just eight, without getting tired. Meditation and yoga are meant for intelligent people of all classes, but they are not of much use to stupid people—of any class.

Q: I have the feeling that you could help me, but I have a tremendous aversion to asking for help or putting myself in a position of dependency. I'd rather remain more limited and achieve all I can on my own than become heavily dependent on a Guru. To me, dependency seems equivalent to personal failure. Please comment.

Baba: If you think intelligently about what you said, you will see that you are suffering from an illusion. You live in God's world, and you don't mind depending on the earth, you don't mind depending on air and other natural elements, you don't mind depending on the food that grows on the earth. You never say to yourself, "I am not going to depend on any of these things." When you are sick, you don't mind depending on a doctor, or if you want to build a house, you don't mind depending on an architect to help you. When this is so, then why does just the Guru stick in your throat?

However your attitude is quite considerate. It seems that you don't want to give any trouble to the Guru, because if you were to depend on him, he would have to worry about you. And you are also leaving poor God in peace.

Q: What is the best way to find a Guru, and how do you know when you have found the right Guru for you?

Baba: First you should cultivate the qualities of a disciple, and once you have done that, you will easily find your Guru. Those people who are deceived by false gurus are exactly those who don't have the qualities of a disciple. They lack aspiration and true longing for liberation. In those cases, taking a guru becomes just a joke.

The more the qualities of a disciple begin to shine through you, the more intense your aspiration, the more quickly will you find your Guru. If a Guru has entered you in the form of Shakti, or energy, that is an indication that you have found your Guru.

Q: When I'm here with you I'm very safe and everything is fine, but I have a problem going to work and working from nine to five in the office. I don't have the supportive environment there that I have around you. How can I deal with this?

Baba: When you leave here, you should carry the state that you experienced here with you into the world; you shouldn't allow your inner state to change when you leave here. Furthermore, when you go out into the world, you shouldn't look at the people out there with doubt or with fear, nor should you consider them to be inferior or low. You should be able to honor and respect people wherever you are. The great sages have described the joy of samadhi as *lokanandah samadhi sukham*, the joy that arises in your heart when you are in the midst of people. You should start looking at them with great love, and then everything will be all right.

Q: What elements of my dharma are important for me to know?

Baba: Your dharma is to do whatever work you are doing and, at the same time, to move progressively toward God. A priest, for example, gives sermons to the people, and it is his dharma to keep doing that. The dharma of a boatman is to row his ferryboat, and a carpenter's dharma is to work with wood. The key element is to remember God also. One's dharma is to do whatever work one can to earn one's livelihood and also remember God with reverence. All the different jobs that are in this world are manifestations of God; so whatever you may be doing will please Him, as long as you do it well.

When a farmer cultivates his land, he is doing God's work, and if he does it well, God feels very happy. When an actress performs, she, too, is doing God's work, and He feels pleased by that. Work and live on the fruits of your labor, remember God intensely, and set a good example for other people—particularly for younger people—so that they may be saved from being drowned. This is the true meaning of one's dharma.

Q: In a competitive, win-lose society, how can one gain a measure of serenity?

Baba: Competition doesn't have any meaning, because you can attain your goal without competing with your fellow beings. Shall I tell you a short story?

Swami Ram Tirth was a great saint of India and a professor of mathematics. One day, while teaching a class in mathematics, he drew a line on the blackboard and said to his students, 'Make it shorter.' Many students ran to the board with their erasers to erase part of it, but Ram Tirth said, 'You must shorten the line without touching it.' The students were taken aback; none of them could shorten it without touching it. The professor then picked up a piece of chalk and drew a longer line just above the first one, saying, "Now, you see, the line has become shorter. So without cutting it down, you can make it shorter." Similarly, you can rise to any height without having to cut another man down. It's only because of deficient understanding that we feel we must compete in order to attain anything.

Q: Baba, could you speak about the proper attitude toward the use of money?

Baba: You should make good use of money. A great Indian saint, said, "You should use your money on good actions. That money should bear happiness and do good for many." Money shouldn't be used carelessly.

Money that is earned honestly and through good actions has the greatest influence. There was a great Sufi saint who used to make hats. It was his daily duty to make two hats. With the money he earned from selling one, he would buy his food, and the money he received from selling the other, he would give away in charity. He remembered God every day and was happy.

A wealthy man used to visit this saint, and since he came every day, his inner being began to change. One day he said, "Look, I have so much wealth. Take it and give up your job."

The saint said, "No, I have to earn my own money. I am strong enough to earn money. I don't want yours. You can give your money away in charity to poor people."

As the wealthy man was going home, he met two people. One of them was lame and the other was blind. He gave some money to each of them in charity, and then he went back to the saint. He told him, "I met two people, one was lame and the other was blind, and I gave them each twenty-five dollars."

The saint said, "You did a very good thing. Now do one more thing. Follow them and see what they do with the money."

He returned just in time to see both of them go into a bar. They hadn't had anything to drink for a long time because they were poor; so they drank a lot there. When they were satisfied they said, "Well, we have never visited a nightclub"; so they jumped into a taxi and went to a nightclub, the rich man following close behind. He didn't like what they were doing. He went back to the saint and told him what had happened.

The saint said, "It doesn't matter; don't worry." The saint took twenty-five cents out of his own pocket and gave it to the rich man, saying, "Give this to the first person you meet on the road. Then follow him and see what he does."

The rich man began to walk down the road and gave the saint's money to the first person he met. With great gratitude, the man put the money into one pocket, and from another pocket, he removed two dead sparrows and threw them away. "For three days," the man explained, "my wife, my children, and I have been starving. I didn't get any work, and we didn't have anything to eat. While I was walking, I saw these two dead birds, so I picked them up. But now, since you have given me twenty-five cents, we don't have to eat dead birds. I will buy some flour with this money and make something to eat from that. Today will go by very well for me and my family."

The wealthy man ran to the saint and said, "Listen, when I gave my fifty dollars away to people, they went to nightclubs, but when I gave your twenty-five cents to someone, he was able to feed his hungry family with it."

The saint said, "Food, clothes, and money imbibe the characteristics of the person who earns them. And those same qualities are passed on with them to others."

That is why you should earn money through good actions and spend money in a good way. To earn money by your own effort is the proper attitude toward money.

Q: For someone living at home—not in an ashram—what would be the essential rules of discipline for living a spiritual life?

Baba: Interior prayer to God or meditation, without any motive or desire, is the most important thing. Keeping the mind free from both hate and attachment is another very important thing. The third important thing that you can do is to eat the fruit of your own work and not depend on others.

Everyone can meditate successfully while living a disciplined life at home. If possible, you should reserve a small place for meditation; just as you have a dining room, a bathroom, a playroom, and so on, likewise it would be wise to make a small meditation room and meditate there regularly.

Q: What is the highest form of love that one can possibly share?

Baba: All that you need to do is to achieve that highest kind of love. You don't have to seek others to share it with. Take a flower, for instance. A flower is not concerned with who will come and smell it. A flower is content to be saturated with fragrance and to permeate the atmosphere with it. You should first attain the highest kind of love and then it will pass to others automatically. The kind of love that includes giving and taking is not the highest kind of love; it is just an ordinary process.

Q: Baba, I know that criticizing and faultfinding are very foolish, and I'm becoming more aware of this all the time, but sometimes I find myself doing this to the people I love the most. Why does this happen?

Baba: You see faults in your loved ones when your love is coupled with desire or selfishness. If you loved purely for the sake of loving and if your love were totally selfless, you would not see faults. Finding faults in others is not wholesome food for the mind. Selfish love arises when you constantly remember all the good things that you do for someone and expect something from that person in return; then you become disappointed when you don't get it and find fault with your loved one. When you stop dwelling on the good things that you do for people, you will find that their faults disappear.

Q: I'd like to know which is more important: devotion to your family or devotion to the Self?

Baba: Both are equal. If you are devoted to your Self, you will be devoted to your family. If you are devoted to your family, you will be devoted to your Self. The highest religion for a householder, which is very dear to the heart of God, is to look at his family with love and reverence. Therefore, we must have great reverence for our spouse, for our children, and for our relatives and friends.

Q: Please describe the roles of the husband and wife in an ideal marriage.

Baba: In an ideal marriage, the husband and wife have a great responsibility toward each other. Each should see the other as divine. The husband and the wife should live together not just to satisfy their sensual desires, but to satisfy the inner Self through meditation. Both of them should be aware of God in all their activities, in attending to every single part of their daily schedule. They should be absorbed in each other and love each other, but that does not mean that they should always be rubbing their bodies together. That kind of love doesn't mean anything.

An ideal spiritual union is one in which the husband and wife have become so absorbed in each other that when the husband eats, the wife is satisfied, and when the wife eats, the husband is satisfied. Each one should live for the benefit of the other; they should not live selfishly. This is an ideal spiritual marriage. In such a marriage, the husband and the wife remain immersed in God all the time. They should be caught in the embrace of pure love and never be able to get out of that embrace. If their awareness is continually immersed in God, the child that comes from such a union will grow into a very great being and do tremendous work in the world. This is the kind of marriage that the scriptures recommend.

Q: Some spiritual teachers recommend sex as an aid in the process of spiritual evolution, whereas others say that one should abstain. What is your opinion?

Baba: The sexual fluid is very valuable. The stronger the sexual fluid is and the more it is retained in the body, the purer and more tranquil the mind will be. The more tranquil the mind becomes, the easier it will be for it to turn inward, and it will also acquire the power to make discoveries in the inner realms.

Seekers can be divided into two categories: total celibates and householders. I am not against married life—in ancient times there were many yogis who were married—nor am I against producing children. But one who is interested in making spiritual progress must conserve his sexual fluid.

Q: Would you please comment on this aspect of spiritual discipline for a married devotee. Should husband and wife strive to live together as brother and sister instead of sharing the same bed?

Baba: A husband and wife do not have to live apart from each other, but it would be very good for them to observe restraint while living together. The Indian medical texts and scriptures say that a husband and wife should observe certain rules in their sexual life; such as having sex only during the post-menstrual phase. Indian medicine says that, while there is happiness in discarding feces, there is happiness in retaining the sexual fluid. Once, a great sage was asked, "How many times should one have sex with one's wife?"

He replied, "If you are seriously concerned about your happiness, then just once in your entire life."

"What if once in one's life doesn't give satisfaction?"

"Then once every twelve years."

"But if that still isn't satisfying, what then?"

"Once every year."

"But if that still is not enough?

"Then once a month, and only during the post-menstrual phase."

"Is it permissable to indulge even more often than that?" asked the seeker.

"Only if you are interested in dying quickly," the sage replied.

If sexual fluid is conserved, it will burst out of you in the form of light, and that will be most satisfying. It is the sexual fluid which bestows radiance, vigor, contentment, and happiness. If you retain it, you become far more attractive than if you lose it. People are deluded in thinking that without sex the husband and wife can't have a happy relationship. In fact, if they had sex less often, their happiness would be much greater, as would their love for one another. The scriptures say that a householder who indulges in sex no more than once a month is a celibate.

The subtle sexual fluid is the same in both man and woman. In the man it is called *virya*, or semen, and in the woman it is called *raja*. A husband likes to see his wife looking radiant, and that glow comes from the preservation of sexual fluid. If the wife loses her glow, it means that she has lost her sexual fluid. A husband feels love for his wife as long as she is radiant, but once she has lost her radiance, he tends to look elsewhere. This indicates that radiance arises from the sexual fluid; so what is more important, to conserve it or to discharge it? A husband and wife should live together and love each other, but they should have sex just once a month. Just as we like to save money and put it in the bank, so we should save our sexual fluid; then we would realize its value. Everyone who follows this advice will be much happier and stronger.

Q: Do you feel that tantric sex is a waste of sexual fluid?

Baba: This is the first time I have heard about tantric sex. People like me stay very far from sex; so I haven't heard about many different kinds.

Tantric sex, mantric sex, sex, sex, sex. You seem to be so obsessed with sex that, even when you go to a holy man, instead of asking about liberation or God, you ask about sex. If somebody could explain to me what tantric sex is, maybe then I could say something about it. There is no such thing as tantric sex in the Tantras.

Q: I have been trying out various teachers and spiritual paths. To experience your teachings, should I repeat your mantra or stick to the mantra I've been using for two years.?

Baba: If your present mantra works for you, stick to it; if not, try mine. It's okay to try out different teachings as long as your goal is to find the one that works for you and to stick to it. Sampling many paths simply for the sake of gathering knowledge is not good.

In Shaivism, there is an aphorism: *Jnanam bandha*—"knowledge is bondage." This means that, if a person acquires too much knowledge about merely how to attain God, it becomes an obstacle to his actual attainment of God.

There was a very great Sufi Siddha called Nakshband Bahauddin. One day a weary seeker came to him and said, "I have been all over the world in search of true knowledge. In one country, I took two courses; in another, six courses; and in still another country, twelve courses. I have studied Sufism, Jainism, Buddhism, and so on. After reading, studying, and even memorizing all the world's great philosophies, I still have not found true knowledge; I have found only fatigue and frustration. People tell me you are a very great teacher; so now I have come to you for instruction in true knowledge."

Nakshband Bahauddin nodded. "It is good that you have taken so many courses and studied so many different philosophies. Tomorrow evening come to my house for dinner." The next evening, the seeker arrived at Nakshband's for dinner and found that the saint had prepared a great feast of almost fifty different dishes, most of which the seeker had never tasted before. As the saint served each dish, he explained, "This is a new kind of curry you must try," or "The sauce on these vegetables is from a very special recipe," and so on, with the result that the curious guest was compelled to sample every course his host offered him, until at last his stomach became very full. Still, Nakshband urged him to eat more, heaping more food on the poor man's plate. The saint also insisted that he sample a great variety of drinks. By the time his host finally told him, "Now, go and have a good sleep," the man could hardly get up from the table.

The seeker went to bed, but couldn't sleep because he had eaten far too much. Within an hour and a half, his intestines began to give him serious trouble. Suddenly, he suffered such an attack of cramps accompanied by so much gas that he couldn't even get to the toilet in time. He lay down again, but before long he had to run to the toilet a second time—he had become like a broken water pipe. All night long he kept shitting and shitting, and in the morning he was so exhausted that he could only lay in bed and groan—"Aaahhh!"

Saint Nakshband went to him and asked, "O brother, how was your night?"

"What can I tell you?" the man said weakly. "All night long I suffered from severe dysentery. It was horrible! I had hoped to attain true knowledge here, but I have attained only dysentery!"

Nakshband Bahauddin told him, "Your experience here happens to be an exact reflection of your spiritual *sadhana*. You have taken too many courses, studied too many philosophies, and visited too many Gurus. And all you have attained is dysentery of knowledge. One who fills himself with too much useless knowledge is no longer open to experience. You must first get rid of all that useless knowledge, then I will show you how to experience truth.''

Therefore, man should choose one path—one diet—and stick to it. The person who eats regularly and enjoys a moderate, sensible diet will never get sick from it. He will always end up feeling satisfied and happy. But those who eat too much from the tables of too many teachers are bound to suffer from dysentery of knowledge.

What makes you think that the supreme truth which you are searching for is hidden in some course or concealed in some philosophy? I once read a poem in Hindi: ''O man! Where are you looking for Me? I am not in temples, I am not in courses, and I am not in philosophies. I am always right within you.''

However, the mind is also right within you, and it's this devil mind which prevents you from recognizing the obvious—that the supreme truth pervades your very own being. When this is so, where else can you go to seek supreme truth? Because of man's only devil—the mind— he wanders here and there, seeking outside for what is right inside his own being.

Give up external seeking. Sit quietly and contemplate your inner Self. If you look within, you will find what you've been searching so long for. The goal you seek is within your own heart, and you can get there only through meditation, not through words.

Q: Is it necessary to practice hatha yoga?

Baba: If the inner Shakti is not yet fully active, the practice of hatha yoga can be very beneficial, as long as you observe the rules of the game. But if you do not, it can become very harmful. There is not much use in practicing hatha yoga anywhere you like, at any time, or learning it from a teacher who is inadequate. What I find is that more people are being harmed by hatha yoga than are being helped. For example, anyone who is very underweight should not do headstands, and those who do the headstand should perform that posture last. After that, one should not do any other postures. At the end of a session to overcome and absorb the fatigue of the different postures, one must lie down in the corpse pose for fifteen minutes. The headstand should follow the corpse pose; then, after the headstand, you should lie down in the corpse pose for another fifteen minutes. No matter how good you are, you should not hold the headstand for more than four minutes.

The scriptures say that a yogi is one who takes suffering away from you; a yogi should not increase your suffering. Anyone who teaches yoga must know all the secrets of this science; otherwise it is dangerous.

Q: Many people in search of spiritual enlightenment put themselves through harsh disciplines, denying themselves many things and giving away all their material possessions. Do you recommend this path?

Baba: Those people who follow these harsh and mortifying disciplines are seeking through self-effort alone. If you were to find a real Guru, there would be no need for such austerities. There was a time when I wandered throughout India wearing just a loincloth, and I led a life of very great hardship. Then I met my Guru, and after I received his grace, I realized that whatever I had done before was unnecessary.

The world is a great friend. Why should we see the world as being antagonistic to us and discard it as an enemy? Those who have discarded it don't really understand what the world is. To experience the Self, or the Atman, which is vibrating in the heart all the time, why should you have to shave your head or give up your home and clothing?

Q: Baba, could you please say something about *tapasya?*

Baba: Always speaking the truth is *tapasya,* and so is not being a nuisance to anyone and not being hostile toward anyone. *Tapasya* means to discipline the mind, which always wanders here and there, by engaging it in the repetition of God's name. The proper self-effort with which you should lead your life is to always be aware of and experience the existence of God in your heart.

The word *tapasya* means "penance," and there are many, many *tapasyas*—some of which are very severe—but these don't have much value. Right in your own home or place of work—you can still do *tapasya* very easily and naturally. The two main goals of all *tapasya* are to empty your heart of enmity and empty your mind of thoughts.

Q: Most ordinary people think that to experience the inner Self, one has to become a monk. Could you talk about that?

Baba: To know your Self, to attain the supreme reality, it is not necessary to become a monk. In India, when people don't want to possess anything or have a family, it is traditional for them to become monks and either wander around or stay in monasteries and instruct others. That's called sannyasa. But one needn't become a sannyasi to have a relationship with God. The attainment of the Self is the same experience for the renunciant and the householder; it is not different.

While remaining in the world and attending to worldly duties, one can still meditate on one's own Self. The world is not at all a hindrance to attaining the supreme principle.

In Maharashtra, which is the western part of India, there have been many people who attained this goal while attending to their duties and remaining in their homes. There was a great Siddha called Kabir, who was a weaver, and he attained realization while weaving. There was another Siddha called Sautamali; while working in the garden, he attained It. Another saint, called Gorakumbar, was a potter, and he realized God while making pots. Another one, called Sena, was a barber; he reached God as he was shaving his customers. They were all great saints, and they all remained right in their own villages and towns. Shirdi Sai Baba remained in Shirdi, a small town in India— throughout his life, he never went anywhere—and he attained It there. He was a very great being. My own Guru, Bhagavan Nityananda, also lived in a small village near Bombay, and he was an omniscient being. So one need not become a monk to realize one's true nature.

Q: How can I get rid of bad habits forever?

Baba: By cultivating good habits. This is why renunciation is necessary. Through renunciation, one can conquer anything. However, this renunciation should not be the renunciation of good habits, but of bad ones; not the renunciation of devotion, but of insensitivity; not the renunciation of purity, but of wanton ways. It should not be renunciation of discipline and regularity, but of lethargy and slovenliness; not of traditional restraints, but of modern license; not of love, but of malice and hostility. You should not renounce the awareness of your greatness, but the mentality of putting yourself down. Don't renounce the inner things, but the outer things. Get drunk on inner brandy, but throw away the outer brandy. Get stoned on the inner LSD of *So'ham,* and throw away the outer drugs; the inner LSD will reveal the Lord Himself. Visit the inner nightclubs, where you will see Kundalini in all Her beauty, and stop visiting outer nightclubs. All that I am asking you to do is to give up external things and turn within to enjoy everything that is inside.

You should be aware that the kingdom of God lies within your very body and think seriously about how to treat this body. You should wear beautiful clothes, keep your hair neat, wash your body with good soaps, and apply perfume. Let God be pleased with the way you respect your body. A lover of God should not look like an abandoned prisoner who has been cast into a dungeon, whose beard is tangled, whose hair is growing wildly, and whose body emits a foul stink. Do not think that renunciation means to renounce beauty and embrace ugliness. The Lord dwells within your body; so you should keep it pure and clean and beautiful.

True renunciation means renunciation of bad things such as anger, envy, jealousy, malice, hostility, and impure habits. However, I am not suggesting that a husband renounce his wife or a wife renounce her husband. I strongly support all legitimate relationships—the relationships between husband and wife, brother and sister, between friends, and so on. They should not be renounced, but enjoyed. You should live a joyful life, but you can only live joyfully through true renunciation.

Q: Do you renounce all personal possessions when you become a disciple?

Baba: Why should you renounce everything? Owning a pencil or clothes or having hair on your head will not prevent you from being a disciple. A woman may have a husband or a man may have a wife, and they may have children and friends, but even that doesn't stand in the way of discipleship. If you have servants or own a factory with a number of employees, that too, doesn't go against your becoming a disciple. A person who has everything is just as acceptable a disciple as a person who is a beggar and has nothing. Discipleship has nothing to do with wealth or poverty. What matters is your heart.

Q: How long should one wait after eating to meditate, practice hatha yoga, or sleep?

Baba: Immediately after eating, you won't be able to meditate very well, because the Shakti is not able to circulate freely when the stomach is full of food. So it is not good to meditate while food is still in the stomach. Meditate before you eat or at least two hours after eating.

For all yogic practices, the stomach should be completely empty. Those who practice or teach hatha yoga should know that one must not practice asanas for at least three hours after a meal; also, one must not eat or drink anything for at least one hour after a session of hatha yoga. A teacher of hatha yoga should make sure his students know this.

The sages have said that we should eat food in the same way that we take medicine, regularly and in carefully measured amounts. To ensure proper digestion, you should fill only half of your stomach with food, one quarter should be filled with water, and the remaining quarter should be left empty, to allow the digestive prana to circulate freely. This way of eating is the sign of a true yogi and is also conducive to living life happily. I read an article about a medical conference in America, at which a famous doctor was asked how much food a person should consume in a day. The doctor replied, "One should eat no more than four hundred grams of food a day. If you eat more than that, you will not be eating for your health, but for your doctor's wealth!" Therefore, exercise control in eating.

You must wait at least two and a half hours before going to sleep so that the food is at least partially digested. The Jains, a religious sect, have a rule that one should not eat after sunset. At first, I thought the rule was absurd, but when I thought carefully about it, I saw that there is some sense in it. What usually happens is that we delay our dinner because of gossiping, and then we eat rather late and go to sleep right after dinner. If you eat before sunset, it ensures that at least three or four hours will pass before you go to bed.

Q: Why should we limit our meditation to an hour and a half every day?

Baba: It's not that you have to limit meditation to only an hour and a half, but you should increase the duration very gradually. Also, the length of time one can meditate is influenced by the strength of one's constitution. If one meditates more than the body can stand, one's head will become too hot. Serious meditators must be sure to eat the right kind of foods. Here in our kitchen, we use cashew and pistachio nuts, clarified butter, raisins, and other such good foods which will give you a lot of strength.

There are many different fluids in the body, but the most important one is called *ojas,* a beautiful, shining yellow fluid that is situated in the bone marrow. This *ojas* is created through semen; it is very radiant, and it gives you the power of memory as well as strength. If we meditate too much and don't give enough rich food to our bodies, the fire of meditation begins to consume the *ojas* from our bones, and we become dull, lose enthusiasm, and become very tired. This is why we have a time limit for meditation.

You can meditate six hours a day if you like, but you have to eat good rich food so that you will have sufficient strength. You will also have to remain celibate, because this *ojas* is created by semen.

If you wish, you can meditate twice a day—one hour in the morning and one hour in the evening—provided that you drink milk and eat sweet things, such as fruit or honey. Even though meditation appears to be very ordinary, it has a lot of power in it; it is like a big fire. In the West, people think that meditation is very mundane and simple, but when you meditate, the fire of meditation burns up all the impurities inside you and makes you completely pure. The more you meditate, the more your body is purified, and if you meditate a lot, you can completely rejuvenate your body, no matter how old you may be. Many ancient sages rejuvenated their bodies in this way, but, practically speaking, to attain salvation or to experience peace, you don't have to do this. However, your mind should become still, and you should become established in your own inner Self. Meditation purifies all your nerves, all your vital airs, and in due course it gives a lot of strength to your body. In the beginning, though, it consumes strength.

Q: Can you tell how far along the spiritual path a person is?

Baba: I can certainly tell how far along the spiritual path you are, but what is the point of it? Everyone, according to his ability, is bound to make progress on the spiritual path, and everybody who is on the spiritual path is bound to reach perfection one day or another. If you are getting good meditations and are really relishing *japa,* it is an indication that you are progressing on the spiritual path. Even if your meditation is not very intense and your *japa* keeps getting interrupted, but your faith in the inner Self keeps increasing, you can be certain that you are moving further ahead. Everything depends on your faith in the Self.

Keep meditating calmly. Have the firm faith within yourself that, "I will do it. I will find what I have set out to find." What you need is firm faith and reverence. Faith is a tremendous aid. One must never lose faith in one's inner Self. You should be aware that you are certain to find it. You should be aware that, just as your bad deeds do not leave you without compelling you to suffer their results, likewise, your good deeds such as *japa,* chanting, and recitation of the *Guru Gita* will produce corresponding fruit.

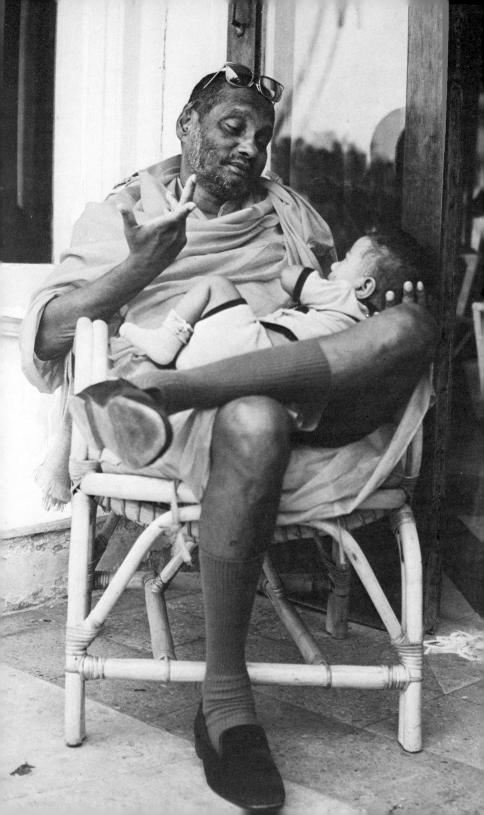

3
MYSTERIOUS ARE
THE WAYS OF KARMA

One of the most persistent questions that people ask regarding the nature of existence is, "Why do some people suffer so much? Why are some rich and others poor; some healthy and happy and others afflicted?" Because we cannot comprehend the laws of the universe, we experience and observe seemingly endless waves of pain and suffering, and we feel ourselves to be victims tossed about at random in a sea of unpredictable events.

When people ask Muktananda about suffering and inequality, he often explains, "A person reaps the fruit of his own actions, no one else's. You are the cause of your own pleasure and pain. You have to bear the consequences of your past actions. An ignorant man suffers them weeping and grumbling, while a wise man, with the eye of knowledge, sees the world as a divine play, as the light of his own soul, and enjoys it innocently."

To illustrate the inevitability of the karmic cycle, Baba tells a true story, which took place during his days of spiritual practice in Bombay.

"A boat called the *Ramdas* was due to sail at eleven o'clock one

morning. Early that day I heard a tremendous racket outside my place.
I went to see what was happening. I saw a man being held by a woman
who was screaming insults at him at the top of her lungs, saying that
he hadn't paid her for three months and was now running out on her.
Her charge was false. The man was a perfect gentleman who lived in
my neighborhood. This was a trick organized by his enemies to insult
him. The police took both the man and the woman to jail, and the
man missed the boat he was to take that day. He came to meet me in
the evening, lamenting bitterly. I said, 'Don't weep. The Lord's hand
must have been behind it.' At five o'clock that evening the news came
that the boat he was to have taken had capsized and everyone was
drowned. But this man was still alive. He came and embraced me. So
you see, one cannot escape the effects of his karma, whether good or
bad. That man's time to die had not yet come, but the others' had, so
that tragedy had to happen.''

The ways in which a Guru influences a disciple's karma are diverse
and intricate. Once a disciple's spiritual energy has been awakened by
the Guru and he begins to meditate, the unresolved impressions of
past actions, or spiritual debts, are reduced and the seeker's future
automatically brightens. At the same time, the Guru guides the disciple in the performance of actions that prevent the creation of new
karma. He also nurtures the development of forbearance and a sense
of detachment so that the disciple is better able to endure whatever his
particular destiny ordains. For his part, the disciple must remain sensitive to the Guru's instructions and fulfill them accurately and with
complete faith.

The subjects of karma and destiny are tremendously complex and
difficult to grasp. In the following talks, interviews, and answers to
questions, Baba Muktananda uses many stories and illustrations to
help seekers understand them.

KARMA AND DESTINY

"You cannot foresee how your karma is going to bear fruit. You may
be quite happy at this moment, but there is no guarantee that you will
be happy in the next. At this moment your good karma may be in
operation, but in the next moment your bad karma may prevail.

"I'll tell you a story. There was a very great devotee of the Lord. He
always remained absorbed in the ecstasy of the divine name and lived

a very clean and pure life. In India, there is a very holy place called Pandharpur, and this devotee often went there on pilgrimages. Once, on his way to Pandharpur, he stopped at a village. It was evening time and he went into a temple sacred to Hanuman and began to chant the name of Rama. Opposite that temple lived a young couple. They heard the sweet voice of the devotee and came over to invite him to their house to eat. The sadhu kept refusing, but the couple insisted. Finally he gave in and went with them to their house. They served him food and drink with great love, and as it grew late they insisted that he spend the night there. The sadhu finally agreed. The husband and wife slept inside the house while the sadhu slept on the porch outside. The young wife was very impressed by the purity of the devotee, and she became infatuated with him. She had a desire to massage his legs and so she went outside to the porch. The moment she touched his legs, her state of devotion changed to one of passion. The sadhu tried to reason with her, to dissuade her from what she was contemplating, but she would not listen. He told her, 'Please go in. I can't touch you. You are a married woman.'

"The woman was so overcome by her passion that she could not think rationally. (This is what the scriptures say also; as soon as you are overcome with passion you lose your ability to reason.) So the woman went inside and, thinking that the devotee would not gratify her as long as her husband was alive, she cut off her husband's head. She came out and told the devotee, 'Now I don't have a husband.'

"The sadhu was shocked. 'Just for a moment's pleasure you have committed such a horrible crime! No, it is out of the question.'

"She became furious and began to scream. The neighbors came running to the house asking what had happened. The woman told them, 'This ruffian! We invited him to our house and fed him with such love, and yet he tried to rape me. When I refused, he killed my husband.'

"The neighbors began to beat the sadhu. But there were some sensible men in the gathering and they said, 'He is a good holy man. Who knows what provoked him to act that way. Let's give him suitable punishment and let him go.' So they cut off his hands and set him free.

"The sadhu resumed his journey to Pandharpur. He was a true devotee. He didn't blame God for the tragic incident; he blamed only his own destiny for what had happened. He continued on his pilgrimage and remained absorbed in the ecstasy of the divine name. By the time he reached Pandharpur, all his bad karma was exhausted. The

Lord then appeared to him and embraced him. The Lord was very pleased with the devotee and told him to ask for a boon. The devotee said, 'After seeing You, I would be a stupid fool to ask for anything else. Nothing in this world is more valuable than Your *darshan*. However, now that I have found such great joy and peace, I do have one question. I want to know why my hands were cut off. I don't want them back, I just want to know the reason.'

"The Lord said, 'Your hands were the only obstacle preventing your union with Me. It was only after they were cut off that that obstacle was removed.' The Lord then touched the sadhu between the eyebrows so that he would experience his past birth. He saw that in his previous birth he was also a sadhu. He saw himself bathing in the holy Ganges offering water to the Lord. Just at that time, a cow came running by. A few moments later a butcher came by and asked the sadhu if he had seen the cow. 'You are bathing in the Ganges; so you must tell the truth,' the butcher said. The sadhu told the butcher that he had seen the cow and pointed out the way. The butcher chased the cow and slaughtered it.

"After some time, that sadhu died and was reborn as the devotee. The cow was reborn as the young wife, and the butcher was reborn as her husband. The sadhu who had directed the butcher lost his hands. The butcher who had slaughtered the sinless cow was slaughtered by his wife, who was the cow in her previous birth. The Lord told the holy man, 'Now you have exhausted your bad karma, and so has the husband. This is how you have to bear the consequences of your karma.'

"Until you have worked out your karma, it will never leave you, no matter how many lifetimes may pass. Therefore, you must be very cautious when performing any particular action. If you want to destroy the bondage of past karma, you must chant the Lord's name very intensely."

GOD'S WILL

"In the *Shrimad Bhagavata*, there is a dialogue between Uddhava and Krishna. Krishna says, 'O Uddhava, strange are the ways of karma. No one can say that any one karma will bear a particular kind of fruit.' Later he says that there is water in all rivers and that, though some rivers are big and some rivers are small, the water is always sweet. But the water of the ocean, which is so vast and unfathomable, is salty.

Who can understand the ways of karma? One gets fruit according to one's karma. Good karmas bear good fruit, and bad karmas bear bad fruit. To erase karmas, one should develop full faith in the Self, remember God, and meditate. Meditation is very necessary. The Bhagavad Gita says that through meditation the fire of knowledge is created, and that fire burns up all karmas so that one becomes free from karmas, free from sins. Then one is able to see God.

"There was a great mahatma who was completely absorbed in love for God. He had a daughter who had reached marriageable age. The saint's wife told him, 'Please go to an astrologer and tell him to read our daughter's horoscope so he can find a very good husband for her and an auspicious time for a wedding.' In India, it is the custom for an astrologer to look at the horoscopes of a girl and boy to see if they're well matched before a wedding is arranged. He also has to check the positions of all the planets to find a favorable time for the wedding.

"The saint's wife asked him repeatedly to find an astrologer, but the saint wasn't very interested in this matter; his sole interest was God. A great sage said, 'When God is taking care of you, who can harm you? Why should you be so concerned about Mars, Mercury, the moon, and the sun?' The saint was so absorbed in love for God that whatever happened didn't matter. He had surrendered everything to God so that whatever action he performed turned out for the best. He didn't want to go out to look for an astrologer, but his wife's constant nagging was obstructing his chanting and worship. In the end, he went to a great astrologer. The astrologer's daughter invited him in and brought him a glass of water. The saint looked at her face and knew that she was a widow. (In India, a widow never applies *kumkum* on her forehead. Some widows shave their heads, too, but not many.) The saint took the glass of water and thought, 'I came here to ask him to find a husband for my daughter and an auspicious time for the wedding, but why should I ask this astrologer when he couldn't predict the future for his own daughter?' He drank the water, said, 'Good morning,' and left.

"As he walked down the street, he came across a lot of people standing in front of a house, weeping and wailing. The saint stood there for a while and wondered, 'Why are these people crying?' A boy came out of the house, and the saint asked him, 'Brother, all these people are crying. What's the matter?'

"The boy replied, 'The man who lives here is the greatest physician in the district, and his only son has died of a terrible disease. That is why people are crying.'

"The saint began to think, 'When I went to the astrologer's house to find an auspicious time for my daughter's marriage, I saw that his daughter was a widow. Now here is a well-known doctor whose son has died of a terrible disease.' He was amazed. As he stood there pondering this, a voice from the sky said, 'Don't worry. Go back to your home. Who can thwart God's will?'

"The saint smiled to himself and said, 'In the astrologer's house, his daughter is a widow. And in the physician's house, his only son died. Who can change God's will?'

"Krishna told Uddhava, 'Mysterious are the ways of karma.' Nobody can change karma; whatever you see is done by God's will alone. A sage said, 'This is the way of karma: A fool becomes a king, a great scholar becomes a nobleman, and an educated person begs for scraps of bread.'

"So a man should try to be steady in pain and pleasure. If something goes wrong, you get angry or upset. But later you should try to remove that feeling and remember that everything happens by God's will. You should remember that. You may not believe it, but it's the truth. A man's intellect is so small—how can that intellect know that everything is done by God's will? Only one whose intellect is developed, one whose mind has opened through meditation or prayer, can perceive this truth."

Q: Is it true that whatever happens is for the best?

Baba: This is true as far as there is truth. Once there was a fakir who was a mahatma, a saint, and he always said, "Whatever God does is for the best." Every day, a king's prime minister used to go to that saint to receive his teachings; so the prime minister also learned that whatever God does is for the best. Now, as prime minister, his advice was often sought by many of the king's subjects. One day, a man came to him and said, "O prime minister, I had a wonderful young son who used to earn a lot of money and take care of me, but a short time ago he died!"

The prime minister said, "I see. Well, whatever God does is for the best."

The man was completely shocked and went away thinking, "What a wretched man that prime minister is! My dear son dies, and he says it's for the best! Anyone else would have consoled me, perhaps even joined me in crying. At least he should have offered me a little money."

A few days later, a woman came to the prime minister and said, "O prime minister, my husband died a while ago, and now I am all alone in the world. I don't know what's to become of me."

The prime minister replied, "Don't worry. Whatever God does is for the best." and that woman went away also feeling that the prime minister had insulted her.

Some more time passed, and another woman came to him, saying, "O prime minister, for a long time I didn't have any children, but finally, a week ago, my first child was born. But just as it came into the world, it died, and now I am very miserable."

The prime minister said, "It's all right. Whatever God does is for the best."

In the course of several weeks, many people came to the prime minister with tales of personal tragedy, and they all got the same reaction: "Whatever God does is for the best." All these people went away very angry with him, and they all wished that something really bad would happen to the prime minister to teach him a lesson for being so insensitive to other people's problems.

One day, the king fell asleep while his royal barber was clipping his fingernails. As the king slept, his arm suddenly twitched, and the barber accidently cut the king's finger, which began to bleed slightly. Immediately, all the people who had it in for the prime minister thought that this was a good time to get revenge. Several people ran to the prime minister, crying, "O sahib! The king's finger is cut, and he is bleeding a lot! There is a lot of royal blood flowing!"

And, sure enough, the prime minister replied, "Whatever God does is for the best."

Everyone ran back to the king and exclaimed, "O Your Majesty! We took the news of your wound to the prime minister, and all he could say about it was that God did it to you, and that it is for the best."

"Is that so?" the king said. "Send him here at once!" When the prime minister appeared before the royal throne, the king said, "I have this cut on my finger. It's still bleeding, and it's very painful. What do you think about this?"

The prime minister said, "O Your Majesty, everything's fine. Whatever God does is for the best."

The angry king shouted, "You rascal! You eat my food and draw a big salary from me, and now that I have been wounded you say that God did it for my own good? Guards! Throw this scoundrel in the dungeon, and give him food only once a day!"

The prime minister was thrown into a dark cell and began to think, "Whatever God does is for the best." So he took advantage of the free time he had and started to meditate.

That afternoon, the king went hunting in the forest. At that time in India, there were some people who believed in making human sacrifices to please a certain goddess, and on that day they had captured a boy for their sacrifice, but he had escaped. Their priest said, "Everything is ready for the sacrifice. Go into the forest and bring back the first person you find. Only be sure that person is completely pure—he should not have the slightest flaw."

The first person they found was the king. They captured him, took him to their settlement, and prepared to bathe him, since the priest had demanded that the person to be sacrificed be completely pure. As they stripped him and began to check his body, they came across the small cut on the king's finger and said, "Look at him! He's been bleeding. Our goddess will never accept someone with such a flaw." So they let him go and began to look for someone else. The lucky king wasted no time in rushing back to the safety of his palace, where he began to think about what the prime minister had said. "If my finger had not been cut this morning, my head would have been cut off this afternoon!" He had his prime minister released and brought to him. "O prime minister, forgive me for not understanding the profound meaning of your words!" And the king told the entire story of his ordeal, and expressed his deep regret for having thrown the prime minister into jail.

But the prime minister interrupted him, exclaiming, "Your Majesty, everything has been equally fortunate for me. If you had not locked me in that dark dungeon, I would have surely gone hunting with you today. After the kidnappers had rejected you for their sacrifice, they would surely have accepted me, for my body doesn't have a scratch on it."

So we should all remember these important words: "Whatever God does is for the best."

Q: Babaji, are Siddhas subject to the law of karma, or destiny?

Baba: A Siddha is totally free, but one doesn't attain the state of Siddhahood through just one lifetime's work. You have to work for many lifetimes.

Look at these pictures; all these beings—Sai Baba, Zipruanna, Nityananda Baba—were all great Siddhas. Food and money used to lie around them in big heaps, but they felt no attachment for them in their hearts. Devotees used to go to Sai Baba of Shirdi with their pockets full of money, hoping he would ask them for it, but Sai Baba would not oblige many of them. He would choose only certain individuals and ask them for it.

I'll tell you the story of a Siddha whose name was Amritrai. *Amrit* means "nectar," and everyone who went to him became filled with that nectar. He always sat majestically on a throne of silver, wearing a turban and regal robes embroidered in gold. Every day he would have a *satsang* like we are having, and people would come and sit in his presence for a while.

No matter where a holy man stays, all kinds of characters come to visit him. There are characters who are just curious to find out what it's all about, there are others who are on the lookout for committing petty thefts, and there are still others who come just for the sake of fun. Only a few would come to Amritrai to seek understanding about the Self.

A Siddha is a very pure being; he is full of renunciation. In fact, renunciation fills his heart all the time. Even in the midst of treasures and wealth, a Siddha lives holding the sword of renunciation right in front of him. To a Siddha, the senses have no value whatsoever. The only thing that has value is the supreme reality, supreme truth.

Amritrai was also a great poet, and one day he sang this song, which he composed: "These possessions are but dust, and no intelligent man will seek them, for they are ephemeral and have absolutely no value." (As he sang this, he was sitting on a silver throne.) "Who will go after fleeting possessions, and why should anyone build these enormous palaces? A humble hut is much better. What need has anyone for majestic royal robes?" (He sang this though he himself was wearing them.) "Isn't it much better to find patches of cloth and sew them into a quilt to cover your body? I feel like going from house to house begging alms for food." (But the fact was that he used to eat from golden plates.)

One man in the audience was quite learned, and he exclaimed, "What on earth are you talking about?"

Amritrai said, "What I am saying is absolutely true."

The man snapped, "It's all right for *you* to talk like that! You sit on a silver throne, you wear royal robes, and you eat from golden plates; so you can easily disdain possessions."

Amritrai replied, "O learned sir, what shall I do? These things are due to my karma. It torments me and will not leave me alone!"

"Is that so?" the man challenged. "All right, come with me tomorrow; we will go for a walk in the forest."

The next day, Amritrai and the scholar found their way to a secluded corner in the forest where they discovered a hut. The scholar said, "I am going to beg for food. Do not leave this place until I return."

On the other side of the same forest there lived a great king who was a disciple of Amritrai's. (Amritrai was the Guru of kings.) Devout kings always kept the vow not to eat their lunch until the food was first offered to fire and then shared with some guest. That day, this king commanded his soldiers and constables to go out looking for a sadhu, a holy man, to be the king's guest for lunch. The soldiers set off on their horses, looking in the forest for a holy man. They came upon Amritrai, who was sitting under a tree by the hut, right where the man had left him.

The soldiers took the Siddha back to their king, who exclaimed, He is the holy Guru! Where did you find him?" And the king put Amritrai on his own throne and, since it was lunchtime, offered food to the Guru on golden plates.

Meanwhile, the scholar had succeeded in gathering a few crumbs of bread and was on his way back to where he had left Amritrai sitting in the forest. He happened to pass the king's camp and spotted the Guru eating in his usual regal manner.

When Amritrai recognized the amazed scholar, he shouted, "O learned sir, see how my karma torments me! Deliver me from it!"

So a Siddha has enormous power and functions in the world according to his destiny. I often visited Zipruanna, who always stayed naked and would always sit around on heaps of filth. All around him you would find at least ten or twenty dogs and pigs, and in the midst of all these creatures, he would be lying peacefully. In India, the tradition is that, if you go to such a saint, you never go empty-handed— you must always take some fruit or sweets or a gift. Whatever Zipruanna received, he would throw to the dogs and pigs, and they would eat it, while Zipruanna remained as tranquil as ever. When I visited him, he would sometimes snatch my bag away, and whatever money was in there he would throw to the dogs and pigs. Then he would tell the animals to eat my money. I would ask him, "What makes you think that dogs and pigs eat money?" He would snap back, "Is it proper for a man to hunger for that which even pigs won't eat?" That was the kind of being he was. He had great power, still he would always recline on a pile of filth. So you can never hope to understand a Siddha's destiny.

Bhartrihari, the great poet-saint, said, "It is impossible to know anything about the ways of perfected beings or to know anything about their karma." Some of them stay completely naked, their only couch is the earth, and they don't even have a torn piece of mattress, whereas some live in royal splendor that surpasses even that of kings. Some are very serene and calm, some stay mute all the time, whereas others never stop swearing, and still others lay around like pythons—they don't even move. If Baba Nityananda, my Guru, happened to lie on one side, he would remain like that for three or four hours before he would turn. One sage said that some Siddhas act like saints, others act like madmen, and still others act like evil spirits, remaining ever in a very strange state. In spite of all this, they are all kings, not beggars.

In Nagpur, there once was a being called Tajuddin Baba. He was a very great saint, and many, many kings would come just to be with him. He had only one addiction, and that was to keep walking around—he was very fond of wandering. One king presented him with a tonga, which is a horse carriage, and another offered him a car, but this being would just keep wandering on foot, and the tonga and the car would follow along behind him. They would also give him very expensive shawls, but he kept the shawls in a bundle slung over his shoulder, and he remained naked; then, as he was walking somewhere, he would just drop the bundle and leave the shawls behind.

Siddhas behave in infinitely different ways. They are most contradictory because they teach scholars and learn from idiots; they fight with heroes and run away from cowards. If people offer them gifts, they renounce everything, and if no one wants to give them anything, they go around begging. In the bitter cold of winter, they drink cold drinks, and in the heat of summer, they eat what we call *sankhya*, which heats up the system. These beings can do anything. Things which appear quite valuable to others appear to be quite worthless to them. The ways of Siddhas are most strange. Siddhas do not play-act—they don't have to—because they are saturated with divine bliss. The senses become their slaves, they don't become the slaves of their senses and live their lives in that wretched slavery. To them, there is no distinction between one's Self and others, between sin and virtue, or between great and small. That is how these great beings live their lives. They may live like beggars, but they are not beggars. They are kings. They are the wealthiest beings. In fact, even the greatest kings beg from them.

Q: Do we have free choice, or is everything that happens in the universe inevitable?

Baba: There is free choice, and it is by means of free choice that you can decide to do good deeds. It is your free choice at present which is making your future destiny, and it was your previous free choice which created your present destiny. Therefore, man is supremely free to exercise discrimination and choose any course of action he wants. You are free to think whatever you want; you are free to have positive and constructive thoughts and wishes.

Q: What part does self-effort play in forming one's destiny, or is even self-effort due to karma?

Baba: Yes, self-effort is also due to karma. In India, there was a great sage, Jagadguru Shankaracharya. He had the courage to raise his staff and proclaim: *aham brahmasmi*—"I am God, everything is God, the whole world is God, God exists within all of you." It took great courage to say that. He was expounding Vedantic philosophy, and now many philosophers follow his system of Vedanta. He was such a great yogi that he could keep his body alive and, at the same time, enter another body.

His ashram was in Shringeri. Once, the king of Vijayanagar went there to meet him. Shankaracharya had malaria and was shivering with chills when the king arrived. One of the ashram officers told the king, "No, you cannot meet Shankaracharya because he has a very high fever."

But when Shankaracharya heard of the king's arrival, he told one of his disciples to bring the king to him.

In those days there were no chairs, so it was the custom to sit on what are called asanas, or low wooden platforms. Shankaracharya invited the king to sit on a wooden asana, and then he told his fever to go and sit on another asana nearby because he wanted to speak to the king. After Shankaracharya transferred his fever into that asana, the platform began to shake violently. The king was astounded. He asked Shankaracharya, "If you can transfer your fever into this wooden asana, why can't you just throw it away?"

Shankaracharya said, "After having become a sadhu, should I now become a thief? I created some karma, and now I have to experience that karma. If I throw my karma away without experiencing it, I am not performing my duty. It doesn't matter what the karmas are—good or bad, pleasant or painful—you cannot escape without experiencing them. However, you can burn up your karma in the fire of knowledge. If you meditate, you are able to light that fire in which your karmas are then burned.''

The *Gita* says, ''The fire of knowledge created by meditation destroys all your karmas.'' Meditation is the self-effort that can improve your destiny. That's why you should meditate.

Q: I have heard that the Guru takes on people's karma at the time he gives them Shaktipat. When you touch seven hundred people during an Intensive, do you take on karma from all of them?

Baba: I don't have to take their karma; it comes to me automatically. A saint has to expect such things. At any rate, all of this karma is burned away within two days. Every morning, I take my bath in the manner prescribed by the scriptures. Then I meditate in a special room, (no matter where I go, I set aside a special room for meditation), and during my meditation, all the karma is burned up. The fire of knowledge of the Self is so powerful that it can burn up any amount of karma. An Intensive may include several hundred people, but this fire of knowledge can burn up the karma of thousands. This is why we accept and worship the Guru, because he does everything for us. He takes away all our negativities. He never takes good things from us; he only takes away what is bad.

Q: When *mahapralaya,* or dissolution, occurs, what happens to individual souls?

Baba: Nothing happens to the souls because only that which takes birth is dissolved. How can that which does not take birth be dissolved? Tukaram Maharaj wrote that the soul is imperishable; so what can dissolution do to the soul? And the Lord says in the *Gita,* ''O Arjuna, the soul is unborn; it is everlasting and eternal. Even when the body is destroyed, the soul knows no destruction.'' If the body is lost, the soul is not lost. Weapons cannot pierce it, fire cannot burn it, water cannot drown it; so what can dissolution do to the soul? Even when dissolution takes place, the soul stays intact.

Q: Is it true that spiritual advancement depends on one's good and bad karma?

Baba: When you experience the inner Self, or God, your bad karma is automatically destroyed. All you need to do is strive earnestly to experience the inner Self. Don't worry about good or bad karma.

It's wrong to think that only after all your karma is exhausted will you experience the Self. It's really the other way around: when you experience the Self, all your karma is burned up. It's delusion to think that when darkness leaves, the sun comes. What actually happens is that first the sun appears and then darkness leaves. When the inner Self is seen, when the inner Self is experienced, all doubts are torn away, the knot in the heart is untied, and all karma is destroyed.

Q: If we eat another person's food, do we take on the karma of that person?

Baba: If you eat another person's food for free, you will surely take on the karma of that person. It is for this reason that when you eat here I make you repeat *Sri Ram, Jai Ram,* and only then can you eat the food. The people who cook here also have to chant; they mustn't gossip.

Once there was a sadhu—a nice, simple man, a righteous person, and a good seeker. While he was traveling around the country, he stopped at the home of a goldsmith. In India, the goldsmiths, no matter how well-off they might be, always steal at least a little of the gold that they use in making ornaments.

This sadhu stayed with the goldsmith for eight days, eating the goldsmith's food and drinking his water; then he left and continued on his way. Later that day, he met a businessman who told him, "Please come to my house and stay for a while." So the sadhu stayed at his house for three days. On the third day, when the sadhu saw the businessman's wife take off her golden necklace and put it into a cupboard, he suddenly felt like stealing it. So he put the necklace into his pocket and quickly left the house.

For the next two days he walked and walked. As no one offered him anything to eat, he finally collapsed beneath a tree and sat holding his head in his hands. He took out the stolen necklace, looked at it, shook his head, and said, "What a sin I have committed. What could have made me do such a terrible thing?"

Retracing his footsteps, he returned to the businessman's house and gave the necklace back, saying, "Please forgive me. I don't know what came over me. Why did I get the terrible urge to steal?"

The businessman said, "There's a very wise man living right across the street. Perhaps he can tell you why this happened."

The sadhu went to the wise man and explained everything that had happened. The wise man asked him, "Whose house did you stay in before you came to stay with the businessman?"

The sadhu said, "Before I came here, I spent eight days in the home of a goldsmith."

"No wonder," the sage told him. "It was eating the goldsmith's food which made you steal the gold necklace."

So this is the effect of food. When you eat someone's food, you should be aware that it carries the influence of whoever gives it to you. That is why we chant a lot before we eat—to purify the food of any negative impressions it may carry.

DEATH AND REBIRTH

Manojit, a student at the University of California, Berkeley, was doing research on death and came to ask Baba how to help people who were dying.

Manojit: What is the death experience?

Baba: You should find out firsthand. There was a great saint in India, Tukaram Maharaj, who said, "I saw my death with my own eyes." In order to have this experience, you must meditate. In meditation you can experience death while you are still alive. To an enlightened person, death is nothing but a kind of sleep. Swamis follow the Hindu tradition very strictly; therefore, when they wake up each morning they must have a bath, because to them sleep is a kind of death, and this is true. The only difference between the two is that sleep lasts for a short time, whereas death lasts longer. So if you are really interested in learning about the death experience, you should practice meditation earnestly. To live through one's own death is one of the essential stages in meditation. In fact, a yogi experiences death before he has a vision of the Lord. There are many students who become so frightened by this experience that they stop their *sadhana* at this point, but there is nothing to be afraid of. I can tell you a lot about death, but it won't be nearly as meaningful to you as having a direct experience of it yourself in meditation. For example, in the *sahasrara,* at the crown of the head, there is a tiny spot of brilliant light, which we call the Blue Pearl. It is the vibration of this light that starts the breathing cycle. In other words, the breathing process derives dynamism from this Blue Pearl. What we call death is nothing but another name for the Blue Pearl's departure from the body. All consciousness is concentrated in the Blue

Pearl; so, when it leaves the body, consciousness also departs—from the bloodstream, from the nerves, and from the breathing process—leaving everything limp and lifeless.

It is sometimes possible to see the soul depart from a dying person. Since you probably haven't had this kind of experience, I will tell you about one of my devotees who once served as secretary of the Ashram. This man devoted most of his time to Ashram work until he developed a brain tumor and was hospitalized. I went to see him, and he told me, "I am about to depart. I have received the final command to leave the body, and it is wonderful that during my last moments I am having your *darshan*."

I asked him, "Is the tumor causing you great pain?"

He said, "No, not at all. I am not even conscious of it. It is only the doctors who tell me that there is a very painful tumor in my brain."

Then I told his wife, "Your husband is about to depart; so take good care of him during his last two or three days of life." He departed three days later, and his wife reported that the last thing he said was, "*Guru Om Guru Om.*" Then she saw the Blue Pearl emerge from one of his eyes and float farther and farther away. She was so fascinated by its beauty that she forgot about the death of her husband; she didn't feel sorrow or grief. The eye that the Blue Pearl had emerged from remained open, but the other was shut.

According to the Upanishads, the aperture through which the soul departs is thrown open as it leaves the body. If it departs through the mouth, the mouth is left open; if it departs through the nose, the nose becomes crooked; if it departs through one ear, that ear changes too; and if it departs through the anus, a lot of shit flows out. These are the various openings through which the soul may leave the body.

Manojit: What happens after the body dies?

Baba: Rebirth takes place. In meditation you can see your past incarnations. You may even be able to see your future incarnations, but that is very rare.

There is a world called *Pitruloka,* where the departed spirits live. St. Theresa describes in her autobiography a visit to this world. If heaven is real, hell is also real; and if heaven and hell are real, this world where the departed ancestors live is also real. If rebirth were not a reality, all the saints would not insist so much on your performing good acts. If the end of this life meant the end of you, what would be the point of subjecting yourself to moral discipline? Even Jesus said, "I have come from the house of my Father, and God is my Father."

If he came from there, he must have gone back there; so that world must be real.

Manojit: How can I help those on the path to die as consciously as possible?

Baba: I am afraid you can't do very much for those who are dying. They have to help themselves. At the time of death, most people become so frightened that they lose consciousness of the outer world and they won't even be aware of you. However, you can pray to the Lord if you like. In the Gita, there is a verse in which the Lord says, "If in your last moment you were to remember Me, you would come to Me." But one does not remember the Lord at that time; one only remembers one's wife and children.

In Indian history there was a Moghul king—a tyrant. He was on his deathbed, but he could not die; all he could do was writhe and twist in agony. Many Muslim priests gathered around him reciting the Koran and trying to explain things to him, but they could not help him. As he lay there writhing and twisting, he told the people around him, "There are three sins that keep staring me in the face at this time. Out of my greed for the throne, I had my father slaughtered. Out of lust, I slaughtered many girls. Then I tried to murder a great Guru, but could not succeed. The memory of these three wicked deeds will not let me die peacefully."

Some people die peacefully, whereas others, because they remember all the bad things they have done, find death very painful. In order to die consciously, one has to perform good acts in one's life. Regardless of the dying person's state, however, you should still chant at his side, and you should pray to the Lord. If the sound of the Lord's name were to find entrance into him, even by force, it would do much good. But you can't help him to remain conscious; one has to earn that by doing good acts. Good meditators pass away in a meditative state, and they are not even conscious of dying.

Manojit: How can I die peacefully?

Baba: In order to die peacefully, you should meditate and remember the Lord. This is the Lord's final word: "If you were to utter My name while leaving the body, you would come to Me." But will you remember to utter His name in the face of the tremendous fear that grips you at the last moment of your life? You will be able to do that only if you have developed the habit of repeating God's name long before the time of your death. That is why the Lord says, "Live your life and continue to repeat My name." From now on, you should become interested in the Lord; then you will die peacefully. I will recite a quotation from a great Indian saint named Bhartrihari, and you should learn this by heart: "As long as the body is healthy and strong, as long as old age is far away, as long as your senses are still able to function, and as long as you still have many years to live, you should work for your spiritual growth by remembering the Lord." You should remember the Lord with such intensity, with such love, that you become permeated by Him long before you die. Otherwise, trying to become addicted to the Lord's name at the time of death would be of no use; it would be just like waiting until your house catches fire before beginning to dig a well to get water for the fire. What's the point of digging the well after the house has caught fire? So in order to die peacefully, you must become addicted to repeating the Lord's name long before you die. And before you can be of any help to others at their time of death, you must yourself chant very intensely and become filled with the Lord.

Q: Do you feel as much joy in contemplating your passage from this life as you feel in living your life?

Baba: Once you experience this inner bliss, it fills you completely. Just as when you cry and lament, you feel great agony and pain inside, when there is an upsurge of bliss within, you become drunk on it. But this bliss lasts; it isn't a brief episode. It stays with you continually, even after you leave the body. Contemplation of leaving the body is as joyful as anything else. In fact, the essence of yoga is not physical exercise but physical death. Real yoga is to die, to experience your own death directly in meditation while you are still alive.

In meditation you get into a state in which you can look at your own death with a serene mind. When a saint dies, he dies laughing. There is a photo here of a naked saint, Zipruanna, who was like a Guru to me. He sent me to my Guru. We were great friends. Though he was always naked, he had total self-control. He was a perfect celibate, and he had unusual powers. He could see far into the future. If I left home to visit him, he would tell people around him, well in advance, that a boy was coming to see him. He acquired such power through yoga that, no matter where he sat—even on a heap of garbage—he would not be defiled. It was as though he were insulated with a protective cover. I visited him a lot.

I will describe to you how he left his body. There was a woman teacher in the village where he lived, and he would occasionally go to her place to have coffee. One morning he arrived at her place around ten o'clock and said, "I must have a bath." This surprised her very much, but she also felt delighted that she was blessed with the opportunity to give a bath to a holy being. Such an opportunity is cherished in India. He had a bath and then he asked that woman to cook a certain snack for him. She cooked it and brought it to him. After he had finished eating, he said, "Zipru is leaving. You can cry to your heart's content." He made a snorelike sound, and that was the end.

This is how a yogi dies. If a yogi could not at least die peacefully, what would be the point of devoting a whole life to yoga? In yoga, before you see God, you must see your own death, and that can be a very terrifying experience. Then, after you have had this experience through inner awakening, death loses its sting, and you see that it is nothing more than deep sleep. In the *Yoga Vasishtha*, which is a great philosophical work, death is described as profound sleep.

Q: In the philosophy I teach, we believe that there is a world we all go to after death. We call it a mental world, and people there are the same as they are in this world, but without bodies. They exist in the mind, and they have to deal with the cravings and desires that they had in the body.

Baba: What you have said is quite correct. What happens is that you leave this life in the same causal body in which you enjoyed profound sleep when you were alive. After your death, you pass into the world of the dead, the world of ancestors. Just as a seed contains the potential for a whole tree, so the soul, when it leaves the physical body, carries with it all its desires and attachments in seed form; they don't disappear. When it is reborn, it is reborn with all those attachments and desires.

Q: In a more evolved condition?

Baba: No, in the same state in which it left its last body. However, after being reborn, the soul can evolve if it wants to. In the interim, between one life and the next, no evolution takes place. It is only in this world that evolution is possible.

Q: Does the mind review the life it has had?

Baba: For quite a while after death, one remains in a state of unconsciousness. Then the spirit wakes up and passes into the world of ancestors. In that world, it is decided where the soul is going to be born next.

There is a central nerve in the subtle body, and it is there that the Kundalini Shakti resides. There, also, you have the impressions of all your past lives. When you are reborn, those impressions are still there inside you. Once your inner Shakti is awakened during meditation, it is possible to see seven of your past lives very clearly, very distinctly; I have seen mine. There is a fort in a section of Maharashtra that I used to visit in my younger days. Whenever I went there, I felt a strange fascination for it, and I would start crying. That fort would draw me to it again and again. I used to wonder why I had such a strong attachment for it; then, years later in meditation, I saw that I had been a king and had lived in that fort in one of my past lives. However, after full knowledge arises within, you don't feel attachment for any of your past existences; I no longer feel any attachment for that fort.

Q: Is there an imminent danger to mankind because of nuclear weapons?

Baba: Without His will, nothing can happen. Let people make bombs; but unless He who has created this world, whose world this is, wills that these bombs should be exploded, they won't explode.

From ancient Indian history there is a story of two brothers, Shumba and Nashumba, who were extremely powerful. They had been granted the boon that nobody in the world would be able to kill them. This happened thousands of years ago. They possessed deadly weapons with which they would rob, beat, and kill everyone they met. The people were sick of those brothers, so they got together and began to pray. From that prayer a deity manifested, and they narrated the story of their suffering to this god. This god said, "Don't you worry. I will take care of it."

This god became the woman Mohini. Mohini means supremely fascinating, supremely beautiful, and one who is bound to enchant everyone. And so this woman went and sat between the two brothers. She first looked at one brother and kissed him, and then she looked at the other and kissed him, and then she stood between the two of them. Now both of them stopped beating and killing other people and they both decided to marry her. She said, "I can't marry both of you; I can only marry one of you."

Shumba said, "I will marry her."

Nashumba said, "No, I will marry her."

They began to fight, and in the end they killed each other. Mohini went back where she had come from.

Who knows what is in God's mind? Who knows what He is going to do in the course of time, and whether these bombs are going to explode? Who knows what is going to happen? So there is no need for man to worry about anything. What he needs to do is to live his life peacefully and also, if possible, to remember the supreme truth.

Q: The present world seems to be on the verge of economic, spiritual, and ecological chaos. Do you think this is the beginning of a new age?

Baba: Time is always changing, and each succeeding moment is a unique one. The world is subject to constant change—sometimes for the better and sometimes for the worse. However, one thing which gives hope and is a cause for great happiness is that young people of today are seeking God and a spiritual life. This is a welcome sign.

Q: One saint remarked that in an age of great chaos the word of God would descend. What do you say about this?

Baba: When there is chaos, it is not only God's word that descends, but God Himself descends. That is what Lord Krishna says in the Gita: "Whenever there is decline in the world, whenever there is chaos and things turn for the worst, I bring Myself forth to set things right." This world is His, its well-being is insured with Him, and it is His responsibility to keep it going. That is why great beings stay calm, because they are full of this certainty.

4
GOING BEYOND THE MIND

A psychologist once asked Swami Muktananda, "What is the basic difference between psychology and Siddha Yoga?"

He replied, "The basic difference between them is that psychology arises from suffering, whereas Siddha Yoga arises from bliss."

The mind is the source of all suffering. Because we don't understand the nature of the mind we are ruled by restlessness, we are pulled here and there by its continual cravings. We are tormented by the recurring anxieties and fears which arise in the mind, but paradoxically, we cling to our minds with tenacity. We do not want, at any cost, to "lose" our minds. But that is just what yogis recommend: to let go of one's desperate grip on the mind, to stop identifying with the mind's activities; to remain tranquil regardless of what the mind presents to upset us.

When people talk with Muktananda, they often express great fear of surrendering their minds in meditation. They are afraid they will lose their minds and go crazy. Muktananda often replies, "You think this because of wrong understanding. Why do you think that God will make you crazy in return for your surrender? On the contrary, He will make you divine. You must get rid of this fear. Whatever is going to happen will happen according to God's will. Why should you be afraid? If surrender to God makes one mad, what a wonderful state to be in. The madness that comes from an experience of union with God is a wonderful thing. What do you gain by *not* surrendering?''

While the psychologist is concerned with trying to understand the mind's activities, a yogi attempts to get beyond the mind to the Self. By simply observing the mind's vagaries and by refusing to become absorbed in them, a yogi is able to witness the inner workings of the psyche and to remain detached from the mind's dramas.

Many psychologists, therapists, and healers come to Muktananda for personal and professional counseling. He has one strong word of caution for these practitioners: therapists who wish to help others should first achieve some sense of peace and fulfillment themselves. One cannot give what one does not have. Muktananda urges these people to meditate, to replenish their own resources, before they attempt to assist others.

Large numbers of professionals have taken this advice. They attend Intensives and come regularly for meditation. These people have related to Muktananda that as a result of their own meditation, their patients are receiving benefits. One psychologist from Macon, Georgia, described his experience: "When I came to Baba, I didn't really know what a Guru was. I thought it was like coming to another therapist. I received Shaktipat, and many extraordinary things began to happen in my life and also in my practice. Now, in addition to my traditional therapy, I give Baba's mantra to the patients and advise them to repeat it. My practice has doubled, and I now have two offices. Not only am I experiencing financial success, but my patients are becoming well. When I was in school, we were told that if we save fifty percent of our patients, it would be good, but now we are saving eighty-five to ninety percent of our patients, and all of those are ones to whom we have given the mantra.''

Dr. Harold Streitfeld, a psychologist and author who experienced inner awakening through Muktananda, devoted several months to traveling around America with him, researching and writing about his own and other people's experience. He brought many of his associates to meet his Guru. One of them told Muktananda that she was afraid to submit to his guidance for fear of losing her individuality. The Swami laughed: "That can't happen. My followers come from all walks of life—administrators, doctors, surgeons, businessmen, politicians, and professors—and they are all functioning very well in the world. They haven't lost anything. You should be aware that the whole universe, animate and inanimate, is a creation of the same Shakti, the same divine energy. So individuality is also a creation of the same Shakti. When that energy is awakened in you, it improves everything; it can't cause any harm. Through surrender, what is small becomes much bigger. If you really want to get somewhere, to achieve divine status, you must annihilate your separate consciousness. It is like a seed that annihilates itself in the soil and then grows into a tree, which bears beautiful flowers and fruit. Unless you surrender your 'selfhood' you cannot attain 'Godhood.' ''.

Muktananda took that psychologist into the meditation room and touched her between the eyebrows and on the forehead. He returned to the *darshan* room and continued his conversation with the other visitors. Some time later, she came out looking quite dazed and happy. Muktananda laughed and said, ''She's got it, and I can assure you that she hasn't lost anything.''

In the following conversations and talks, Baba Muktananda reveals his extraordinarily subtle understanding of psychology, the mind, and the mantra. He encourages students of psychology to meditate and to repeat the mantra in order to go beyond the mind, and to experience the Self.

Swami Shankarananda and Mother Girija, long-time devotees of Muktananda, founded an Ashram in Ann Arbor, Michigan. Muktananda visited there soon after the Ashram was opened, and during that visit a group of psychology professors and students from the University of Michigan came for satsang.

Baba: I have encountered many students of psychology all over the country. I gave lectures at Stanford University and Sonoma State College, and I also attended a conference of humanistic psychologists in San Diego. I have observed that the mind seems to be a problem for everyone. Whether one is rich or poor, his mind gives him a lot of trouble. A learned man is not satisfied with learning, but he does not want to be stupid either. Some people become sick of pleasures and enjoyments yet they don't develop a desire for renunciation. A woman isn't happy being a woman, and a man isn't happy being a man. The mind behaves very strangely; it becomes unhappy even when one has everything. The mind seems to torment everyone. It is fickle and changeable. It seeks the company of many kinds of people but not of God.

Since ancient times, there have also been many psychologists in India who have been involved with the study of the mind. As a result of their studies, we have many rituals and methods of worship that are meant for the purification of the mind, and they are becoming popular even here in the West. The goal of our sages and seers was to still the mind, free it from passions, and stabilize it. Our ancient seers taught that it does not matter if one doesn't have enough clothes to wear or enough food to eat, but one must become free from the perversions of the mind. An agitated mind produces suffering even in the midst of affluence; it doesn't seem to know how to become quiet or still. This is the reason that our ancient sages and seers were involved with yoga, meditation, and right knowledge. They tried to find ways to still the mind, to make it steady, and to free it from all its impurities and defects and thus live their lives in happiness and joy. If one could attain the state that is free of all thoughts through meditation, one would live one's life peacefully. I have told you about the goals of our sages, and now I would like to hear from you.

Professor: You said that it is possible to live one's life peacefully through meditation. Is that true for Americans like us, whose lives are full of distractions? Or would we have to change our lives in order to meditate successfully?

Baba: You don't have to change your lifestyle. I have been traveling through different countries, and I haven't found much difference in the lifestyles of people. No matter how busy your life is, that in itself is not an obstacle, but your attitude can be an obstacle. It is quite possible for a man to develop what the Bhagavad Gita calls the power of the intellect, or the power by which one can function effectively even in the midst of unfavorable circumstances. As far as distractions are concerned, they will always be there. But if you can attain the power of wisdom, the power of a cultivated intellect, you will be able to work even more than before, regardless of circumstances.

Professor: Where does meditation come in? Is it a daily routine that we must adopt?

Baba: Just as you eat every day, sleep every day, earn money every day, acquire possessions every day, go to work in the factory or office and return home every day, likewise it would be good to meditate every day. If you can do everything else daily, you can certainly meditate every day also.

Professor: Does each individual have his own meditation, or is there one meditation that is appropriate for all people?

Baba: The essence of meditation is to make the mind totally still, and many different techniques have been recommended for that; but it is the stillness which is important. Regardless of what techniques one follows, one's mind should become purer and steadier. There are many people who would prescribe different meditation techniques, but the true meditation is that which arises from within spontaneously.

Professor: Do you need a teacher to awaken this spontaneous meditation?

Baba: Yes, that is very, very necessary. A Guru who can activate spontaneous meditation in you is a very high being; you cannot be cheated by such a Guru. Such beings are very rare, and if you can find one, it is a great blessing. Spontaneous meditation does not cause any harm. In fact, this form of meditation leads you to the state of perfection. It is the best kind of meditation. The kind of meditation that you do through techniques, through your own effort, is very ordinary. Besides, spontaneous meditation includes all different forms of meditation and yoga, and one doesn't have to run around thinking that he needs to try every new course and technique.

Student: I understand that you have reached the state of nirvana. I would like to know if it is something you spent your whole life trying to achieve, or is it something that just happened one day, like spontaneous meditation.

Baba: The state that I have attained is within everyone. Many years of my life were spent in quest of it. Actually, there are people who spend not just many years, but many lifetimes practicing different techniques in their quest, and yet nothing comes into their hands. However, if you could find a perfect being like my Guru, Nityananda, and obtain his grace, you could have a direct personal experience of that state in an instant.

Student: So it doesn't matter what form of meditation you do, but rather what teacher you get it from?

Baba: Yes, that is totally correct. I practiced so many different techniques and studied so many different scriptures, yet none gave me the experience I desired. It was only after receiving the touch of my

Guru that I attained what I was looking for, and then I actually realized the truth of all the scriptures that I had studied and also attained the goal of all the techniques that I had practiced.

Student: Since I met you, I have worked through many things in my mind that I was unable to work through in psychotherapy, and I wonder how this is possible.

Baba: It is due to the power of Nityananda's touch. Even psychiatrists cannot impart that touch; only a rare being who has arrived at the place beyond the mind can give you this touch. All the experiences you are having are due to inner awakening, to the subtle yoga which is going on inside you as a result of that touch. This inner touch also cleanses the impurities of the mind.

This is what you may call easy yoga; it is also known as Siddha Yoga or yoga of Shaktipat. This takes you to the other side of the mind. There was a great yogi, Jnaneshwar Maharaj, who was called king of all yogis. He used to say—and this is a good one for psychologists—"O my mind, why don't you enjoy that which remains when the mind ceases to be mind, when the mind merges itself into the highest truth, the supreme truth?" So why don't *you* remain aware of that which remains after the mind ceases to be mind?

Student: Is it not enough to have perfect faith in oneself? What else do you need?

Baba: It is great to have faith in yourself, but unfortunately people find it easier to put trust in everything else. If someone told you that the highest energy dwells in water, you would believe him and rush to find some water. If someone told you that the highest energy dwells in fire, you would believe him and rush to find fire. But if someone told you that the highest energy dwells within you, you would say, "How can that be possible? I am inferior; I am a sinner." The whole purpose of meditation is not to attain God, but to develop this faith in your own Self. God has always been inside us, and it is only because of lack of faith that we haven't been able to experience Him. Faith has great power. To have faith in your Self is the greatest good that you can do for yourself.

Professor: In our college we have a meditation room where we do biofeedback, teach meditation, and study altered states of consciousness. How can we best continue our work?

Baba: What you are doing is quite valid. However, if you want to do better work, you should investigate the nature of the mind directly, through meditation. What is your understanding of the mind?

Professor: That is a very difficult question. One way of speaking about the mind is to say that the mind is just a piece of some larger portion.

Baba: This is what we say also. The individual mind is a portion of the universal mind. According to yogic psychology, the mind is nothing but Chiti—universal Consciousness or divine energy. It is not inert. This universal energy becomes the mind. There are two states of consciousness: contracted or limited consciousness and expanded consciousness. Psychologists are not in a position to talk about these two states; only yogis can talk about them. It is only in the contracted state of consciousness that we are caught up in the mind. In the expanded state of consciousness, the mind is not experienced as the mind. It is experienced as expanded consciousness. So there is really no such thing as the mind. One saint asked another, "Who is God?" The second saint replied, "The one who is the witness of the mind."

Right now we are trapped in the mind, but if we could go beyond it, we would understand not only the nature of the mind, but also the nature of the world and our own true nature. King Janaka asked the sage Yajnavalkya about God and the nature of the mind. Yajnavalkya said, "God is the being who lives behind the mind and makes it move, who cannot be known by the mind, and whose body is the mind. He is the sole indweller. He is immortal. He is purest bliss."

Therefore, people like you should try to go beyond the mind. I have much respect for the work psychologists are doing in America. I call upon all of you to try meditation, not for the sake of yoga, not even for the sake of liberation, but as a means to investigate the nature of the mind. There is a most wonderful divine energy within, and if psychologists could tap that, they could do a lot of good for the world.

Groups of psychologists, psychiatrists, and therapists often visit Muktananda to discuss problems of the mind. One such group of about sixty psychologists met with him in New York City at a program arranged by Dr. Harold Streitfeld.

Dr. Streitfeld: Baba, I have found you to be a master therapist. I have witnessed and experienced a kind of mysterious psychotherapy that begins to take place within as the process of spontaneous yoga unfolds under your guidance. You have the intuitive power to know exactly what is needed by a person at a given time and what will be a challenge to him in his personal and spiritual growth. You can do this with hundreds and hundreds of people. How do you manage this? Your timing is extraordinary. We therapists see only a small number of patients, and yet we need to make detailed records in order to keep track of all of them. Baba, you have thousands and thousands of devotees, and you never take notes. How are you able to keep track of them and of all their needs and problems?

Baba: If you have a thorough knowledge of every kind of sickness, you will find that any particular sickness will itself tell you what treatment to prescribe for it. A therapist or a doctor has to be aware of two things: disease and its remedies. Good doctors have a kind of inner meter by which they can detect diseases, and it is this inner meter which is important. The moment a patient comes in front of you, you can tell what the illness is and what the remedy should be. Every therapist should try to acquire this inner meter.

HS: And not let your thinking get in the way?

Baba: Eventually, even the mind takes on the character of that inner meter, and then the mind doesn't get in the way. It is only as long as the mind keeps roaming outside and becomes involved in outer objects that it is the mind as we normally know it. But when it turns within totally, when it is dissolved into Consciousness, the mind itself becomes that meter.

HS: Isn't it hard to work after the mind has dissolved?

Baba: Don't take that expression literally. I don't mean that the mind ceases to function or that one loses consciousness. Just as water acquires the color of anything it comes in contact with, so does the mind. When the color of water changes, the water does not cease to be water. Similarly, when the mind merges into the inner Self, it doesn't cease to function; it is not destroyed. Some people have an irrational fear in this regard because they don't understand what the phrase "dissolution of the mind" means.

What is the nature of the mind? It is not an inert substance but the energy of Consciousness itself. When that energy is directed outward, it becomes what we call the "mind." When it turns inward, into itself, then we say that the mind has been dissolved. Our sages have defined the supreme reality, or Consciousness or the inner Self, as that which, though it lives in the mind, is separate from the mind. It cannot be known by the mind because the mind is its body. It makes the mind active. It is inner Consciousness, the purest joy. As long as that inner Consciousness functions, a therapist need not fear that the mind will cease to function.

Psychologist: How do we help the man who sees everything in a negative way?

Baba: By being friends with him, and by giving him your love and approaching him through your heart. But first it is necessary for one to totally help oneself—to unfold all the strength there is inside. It is no use trying to help others if you haven't helped yourself. What we need to do first is to become stronger ourselves and discover the power of the Self within. Then, by means of goodwill and the inner power, we will be able to help others.

I have also studied medicine—the Indian system of Ayurvedic medicine, not Western medicine. According to Ayurvedic medicine, a doctor's love for his patients is far more effective than medicine. According to our medical texts, a drug is only forty percent important, whereas a doctor's love and his goodwill for the patient is sixty percent important. At one time, I practiced Ayurvedic medicine, but I gave it up because I realized that there were many others doing the same work and that if I quit it would be no loss to anyone. Even now I occasionally recommend Ayurvedic medicine, but my principle work is to prescribe medicines, not for physical ailments, but for the disease of existence, which is more harmful than all other diseases put together. Other diseases afflict only the sick, but this disease afflicts even healthy people.

Physician: Do you see disease as a symptom of defects in the spirit?

Baba: Generally speaking, a disease results from the combination of two factors—the wrong kind of food that the body eats and the wrong kind of food that the mind eats. Our Ayurvedic system of medicine says that you should take food like medicine. It is food which keeps you healthy and ensures longevity, and it is also food which can make you weak and feeble if you eat indiscriminately. And when I say that the mind eats the wrong kind of food, I mean that it thinks all kinds of negative thoughts like anger, jealousy, greed, lust, or anxiety.

Psychologist: Sometimes we work with people who are very disturbed, and their disturbance reaches a place inside us where we are ourselves disturbed in the same way. I wonder how, when working with such patients, we can open ourselves up to them while not taking in things that are not good for us?

Baba: Healers or therapists sometimes do absorb the negative influences of their patients. In many cases it happens that they start out as therapists and end up as patients. In San Diego, California, I attended a large convention of humanistic psychologists. A woman healer came up to me and said, "When I started, I was doing good work and helping people, but now my arms and legs have begun to ache terribly and are nearly paralyzed. What should I do?"

This is a common complaint of therapists and healers who have come to see me. And this is exactly what happens to me, too, when I give Shaktipat. At an Intensive I may touch as many as six hundred people, and the impurities and sicknesses of those people come into me. It pains me quite a bit, but afterward I sit quietly in meditation. and through the force of the divine energy that is released in high meditation, I am able to burn up all those negativities. This is how I stay fresh.

Therapists and healers should also find a way to burn up the impurities they absorb from their patients. It is not enough to become drunk on your temporary success as a healer. You must think about the future and what may happen to you as a result of your healing work. It is essential for a therapist to be in touch with his inner energy and to keep himself strong.

Another thing I would like you to be aware of is the fact that the sickness a patient suffers from is a result of his karma, and it has to be endured. Who will endure it? If, in the name of helping other people through healing, you rid a person of his sickness, what will happen to his karma? It will come into you. I once read the true story of a judge. While he was delivering a verdict, he mistakenly awarded a sentence of thirteen days instead of the fifteen days called for by law. Afterward, he became conscious of the fact that he had made a mistake; so he himself went into prison for two days to suffer the prisoner's remaining karma.

I am not suggesting that you should stop helping patients, but it is good to be aware that whatever sickness comes to a person is a result of his karma. In the Mahabharata it is said that you must suffer the consequences of your karma; there is absolutely no escape from it. Your karma will keep chasing you until you have suffered it. And if, as a healer, you try to free a patient from his karma, his karma will come chasing after you. Therefore, it is necessary for a healer or therapist to first acquire sufficient spiritual power to burn up his patient's karma by means of prayer. Or you can unfold your own inner power through meditation and set ablaze the fire of yoga inside you to burn up your patients' negative karmas.

Psychologist: What is the relationship between prayer and psychic healing?

Baba: When you are healed through prayer, it is the power of speech at work. But there is only one energy in the universe, and it keeps expressing itself in different forms. The same power of speech can hurt a person as well as heal him. So it is the same Shakti, the same energy, which is at work everywhere. It is that energy which is the healing power even in medicine. It also produces illness if you eat things that don't suit you. So if a healer's motives are pure, the same Shakti will help him to help others. There is great power in prayer to God. By means of prayer, any amount of good can be done.

Psychologist: Could you speak about the connection between surrender and healing?

Baba: When your surrender becomes perfect, you become a perfect healer. The farther away you are from surrender, the less effective you are as a healer. A healer needs surrender very badly; so you should understand the true meaning of surrender. Surrender means becoming one with that power which is great and vast. It doesn't mean considering yourself to be small and inferior or becoming a pitiful, helpless person. Surrender means to merge yourself with God. Through surrender you absorb God's energy in its fullness.

Gerry Nash, a psychiatrist at Napa State Hospital in northern California, came to see Muktananda in Piedmont. He related a dream he had the week before in which he saw the Swami and other people sitting in a room similar to the darshan *room where he now sat. He asked the meaning of this dream, and Muktananda answered, "People who are pure can see future happenings in dreams. You must have seen this very room."*

Gerry Nash: A lot of psychology is based on an atheistic approach. Most sciences do not take universal Consciousness into account. Only lately have studies been undertaken to confirm the hypothesis of a power that includes everything; yet there is not a scientific school of thought that allows for this.

Baba: Yogis just grab hold of the mind and put it in its place. This shows that there must be a power that is stronger than the mind, a power that can grab hold of the mind. Now, the question is: Who knows how the mind functions? Who watches the thoughts passing through the mind? It cannot be the mind itself. If you say that there is another, higher mind watching this mind, there must be yet a higher mind watching the second one, and a fourth mind watching the third, and so on. This is Vedantic philosophy.

Therefore, psychology should accept the existence of a power superior to the mind. There is somebody inside you who tells you, "Look, your mind is not in good shape; your mind is restless." And it tells you, "Now your mind is at peace; your mind is full of happiness." That somebody cannot be the mind. That being inside must be different from the mind.

GN: Sometimes it does seem that there is a witness that is separate from the mind and can watch the mind do its tricks. But at other times the mind seems so powerful that even the witness gets caught up in it.

Baba: The ordinary mind cannot go anywhere near the witness. If the mind does get close to the witness, it merges with the witness. Suppose that you stand for the mind, and I am the witness of the mind. I can watch you only if you are at some distance from me. If you were to come too close to me, you would no longer be an object of perception; you would become one with the seer.

GN: Then it's not possible for me to merge my mind with that witness?

Baba: For that you will have to study our scriptures. You will have to study *my* psychology—the psychology of meditation. The witness of the mind has to be different from the mind. The inner witness lives in the mind but is apart from the mind. The mind is the vehicle of the witness, and therefore it cannot also be the driver of the vehicle. The inner Self makes the mind think, but it cannot be known by the mind.

GN: Since we are operating through the mind, how can we ever hope to comprehend the witness?

Baba: The witness continues to exist even when the mind ceases to exist. It is the highest reality, and psychologists should try to experience it. But most psychologists will find it very difficult to get to that place because they are accustomed to working at a point which is quite far away from the witness. If you want to get to that place, you will have to work at it a little, like we do. You will have to meditate and follow discipline in your life.

GN: My discipline seems to be changing. I am working in a mental hospital with people whose minds are running here and there. It is difficult for me to remain centered while helping those people because I am very susceptible to the wanderings of their minds.

Baba: You could do your work quite easily if you would become firmly centered in witness-consciousness, which means to function with one's awareness centered, not in the mind, but in the witness beyond the mind. Once you become established in the inner witness, things outside you do not have much effect on you. The mind is subject to all kinds of thoughts, desires, and passions, such as anger, greed, lust, pride, vanity, conceit, delusion, and fear. Since the mind can be attacked by these passions at any given time, there is always bound to be agitation in the mind; but these mental agitations can never go anywhere near the witness. The witness remains untouched. Delusion and attachment cease to exist for one who has become centered in the witness, the Self.

GN: I don't mind giving up greed, lust, and anger, but the positive emotions still attract me.

Baba: To become centered in the Self doesn't mean that the positive things will be destroyed along with the negative. Love, faith, and happiness will remain in even greater measure than before.

GN: Is there one universal Consciousness?

Baba: Yes.

GN: Would this be a universal mind?

Baba: Yes, and it is supremely pure. The individual mind springs from the universal mind but remains connected to it. The two minds function differently. The individual mind functions from ego-consciousness, but the moment ego-consciousness disappears the individual mind becomes the universal mind.

GN: Are you saying that the ego-consciousness is the witness?

Baba: No, ego-consciousness is just a mental attribute. It is a manifestation of the inner witness, but it is not that witness. In ego-consciousness, our sense of "self" is tied to the body and mind, but in the state of enlightenment, it is not attached to those things; it is merged in the universal Self.

GN: Is this the object of meditation?

Baba: Yes, the object of meditation is identification with the inner witness.

In Los Angeles, David Zeller, a humanistic psychologist at Johnston College, came to speak with Muktananda.

David Zeller: I would like to talk to you about the heart. In terms of my own work as a teacher and my own growth, I want to know what can be done to open the heart. I feel that so many of the schools teach from the head, not from the heart, and I want to work through the heart.

Baba: Meditate. The inner Shakti should be awakened through meditation. When the inner Shakti becomes awake and opens the heart, you become aware of exactly what the heart is. There is no point in teaching theoretical knowledge or concepts about it to people. There are many different powers inside man and when they become active through meditation, you will be able to experience all of them. One of the powers enables you to hear distant sounds, and another reveals the past and the future. You should experience all these through meditation. Meditation is the main thing.

DZ: I feel that the heart is the place where all other centers become integrated. I don't want to teach theoretically; I want to teach from the heart because I feel that is the only way to teach.

Baba: For that you should meditate. Through meditation you should be able to get to the place from which the ego arises and into which it subsides. Find the place from which all the different thoughts of the mind originate—that is the heart.

DZ: Is there a special meditation that is best for the heart?

Baba: The meditation that you get through Shaktipat is the best because it is the meditation which arises spontaneously after Kundalini awakening and inner unfolding.

DZ: We try to teach transpersonal psychology, yet none of us are really ready to teach. Any guidance that you could give us would be appreciated.

Baba: There is no point in giving mere verbal advice. You should meditate; that is the best advice I can give. Many professors come to meet me, and I tell them the same thing. More and more people are accepting the idea that there is something beyond the mind, and I tell everyone to meditate in order to experience that.

DZ: We agree. The question is how to perfect this within the framework of a college institution. We don't have the facility of an ashram, yet we want to do something.

Baba: All of you will have to learn to meditate somewhere else. Just as you go to an institution to receive your degree, so you must go to an ashram to learn meditation. In other words, you have to go where meditation is taught, or you can make a temple of meditation in your own home.

DZ: How do I deal with the fear, in myself and in people around me, of having to let go of more and more as the process of meditation and awakening unfolds?

Baba: One should keep meditating because the blocks one has will disappear through meditation—they will dissolve. Meditation will unlock them.

DZ: But what about the fear of going crazy or losing control of the things in the world that we try to hold on to?

Baba: You don't have time to go to an ashram, you don't want to come down from your position as a professor to learn humbly at the feet of great teachers, nor do you want to go crazy. Should we make some meditation pills and sell them in the market? There is a certain way to learn a certain thing. Whether you are an Indian or an American or a European, you have to learn it the way it is taught. Boys from India come to America to learn engineering, and they have to learn it the way it is taught here. They can't dictate their own terms by saying, "We want to learn it in the Indian style." Meditation, like any other science, is not limited by language, race, religion, or nationality. It is a universal truth; but you must learn it the way it is taught.

DZ: Isn't it possible to practice both at the same time? Do we have to live totally in an ashram, or is it possible to pursue spiritual life in the world?

Baba: Yes, it is possible to combine both. You can meditate while you are doing your work. In India, most people who meditate do not leave their work for meditation. Meditation will never go against your daily life in the world. In the West, also, I have met many very good meditators who meditate while continuing their work. Some of them are professors and some are teachers; others are military officials, businessmen, and judges. Many students also come to our Ashram. They are all very good meditators, and none of them have given up their work. Why don't you attend an Intensive with us?

Q: If the body is just inert flesh and the soul is pure Consciousness, what is it that experiences pleasure and pain?

Baba: This is a very important question. It would seem that the person who asked this question has experienced pleasure and pain. You should try to find the answer to this question yourself, when you are experiencing these feelings, but at that time you always forget to inquire who the experiencer is and begin to question only afterward.

The body is completely inert. If it could experience pleasure and pain, even a dead body could feel these things. In India, corpses are burned on pyres, but not even a single body has ever cried out in pain as the fire consumed it. So this proves that the body itself does not have feelings.

Furthermore, the Self, or the soul, is so pure, clean and clear that neither pleasure nor pain can reach it. So if neither the body—that is, the senses—nor the Self experiences pleasure and pain, then who or what is experiencing these things?

Even though the body is inert, it is able to function because of the Self, which activates it through what we call the *antahkarana,* the four psychic instruments of ego, mind, intellect, and subconscious. Through these four psychic instruments shines the light of the Self. In this way, the body becomes conscious, and pleasure and pain are experienced.

The *antahkarana* is like a lens or magnifying glass. If we keep such a lens inside our house, nothing will happen—the lens cannot cause us any harm. But if we place it on the roof where the light of the sun passes through it, it can cause a fire that will consume the entire house. Who should we blame for causing this fire? The lens is blameless because it is completely inert. The sun, also, is free from blame. Only because the light of the sun falls upon this lens is fire created. In the same way, the *antahkarana,* when illuminated by the light of the Self, creates and experiences pleasure and pain. Therefore, that which is between the body and the Self is what enjoys and suffers. Yogis meditate to transcend this *antahkarana* and attain a state that is free of both pleasure and pain.

Q: Why does the mind play tricks on us? Why don't things appear to us in their pure form?

Baba: The mind plays tricks when it sees that you are weak. But if the mind were to see that you are centered in the Self, it would become your slave and lie at your feet; it would no longer play tricks on you. The mind plays its tricks as long as we are subject to the six passions, the six enemies: lust, infatuation, grief, jealousy, greed, and anger. But once we are purged of these passions, the mind stops bothering us.

There was a seer, a man of firm resolution. He always did what he said he would do. One day he took a sip of holy water and resolved, "I am going to stop all the thoughts and fancies of my mind, I am going to give another direction to my fantasies, and I am going to become absorbed in meditation."

After a while, a figure came out of his body, stood right in front of him, and said, "I am leaving."

The seer said, "Who are you?"

The figure said, "I am your mind. Now that you have decided to stop all fancies and thoughts, I have to find some other place to live. If you won't let me influence you, why should I stay with you?"

Then another figure came out and stood in front of him. The seer asked, "Who are you?"

He said, "I am your imagination."

"Where are you going?"

"I'm moving away from you. If you will not get caught in the grip of my fantasies, why should I stay with you?"

The mind plays its tricks on you because you have become friends with the mind, because you have become a slave to the mind. If you become centered in the Self, if you become free, the mind will just lie quietly.

Q: I often have difficulty with anger and am unable to control myself. Some people say that one should not suppress or curb these feelings, but if I don't, I have to vent my anger on someone.

Baba: The people who say that one should not control one's anger are mistaken. If you immediately curb the feeling of anger when it arises, it is changed into a feeling of love. By suppressing the feelings of sexual desire, anger, attachment, and greed, they are transformed into their opposites. If one doesn't control anger, it keeps growing.

Q: Where does the anger come from?

Baba: According to the Gita, anger is born when a desire is not fulfilled. Anger is not to be cherished. One should first understand it and then get rid of it. Some physical disorders can also lead to anger, such as the presence of too many toxins in the bloodstream. Anger also arises when things seem to go against your inclinations. Anger is not good. Why have you asked this question?

Q: Because I have spent the greater part of my life being very angry. But recently I have begun to think that there must be a way to refuse anger.

Baba: Discrimination is the way. Through right discrimination, anger can be overcome. This is what the Gita says. As anger arises again and again, one should fight it with discrimination and thus destroy it. Pray intensely to the Lord, and that will take care of your anger.

Q: Pray to not be angry?

Baba: As you pray to God with more and more love and respect, anger subsides. When your love for God increases, anger decreases.

Q: Until that happens, what should I do when I am angry?

Baba: Become silent

Q: That is very hard.

Baba: It is not easy to overcome anger.

Q: Anger takes over.

Baba: Don't allow anger to take charge of you.

Q: Anger doesn't seem to need my permission.

Baba: You have to allow the peaceful side of your mind to work on the anger.

Q: When I am angry, sometimes I say things I don't want to say and do things I don't want to do. There is nothing rational about it.

Baba: That is what happens; then, later, one is filled with remorse.

Q: And exhaustion.

Baba: There is only one way to overcome anger and that is to pray to the Lord and repeat his name continually. One should repeat the name of *Rama* over and over; that is the only way.

Q: Especially at times when I am angry?

Baba: Even more so at those times; do it very intensely.

Dr. Streitfeld brought a group of eminent psychologists to the Oakland Ashram to discuss meditation and its role in psychotherapy. Muktananda was very happy to learn that they were recommending meditation and the use of mantra to their patients.

Psychologist: I would like to talk about meditation in order to get a clearer understanding of it.

Baba: The practice of meditation is not the goal of meditation. Only after constant meditation do you reach the goal. The scriptures on meditation say that you should reach a state of thoughtlessness, and that is the culmination of meditation. The nature of the mind is to think constantly about one thing or another; true meditation is the state in which the mind becomes thoughtless. Even in our normal, everyday existence a man may become stunned, or thoughtless, when, for example, he is overpowered by a feeling of deep emotion such as love or anger. But that state is brought about by the force of circumstances. One should be able to experience such a thoughtless state quite naturally; that is the goal of real meditation.

Psychologist: In our work, my associates and I suggest meditation to our patients who are too anxious or nervous. We have found it to be valuable therapeutically.

Baba: It would be very beneficial for your patients if you introduced them to meditation and mantra.

It seems that doctors have done some research on this matter and have found mantra and meditation to be beneficial for treatment of heart disease and other ailments. But actually there is no need to do a lot of research. If you just sit in a corner quietly and repeat the mantra for a few minutes, you will have an immediate, firsthand experience of the effect of the mantra. It is subject to immediate verification. Mantra, as well as meditation, will be of immense help to you in treating patients.

Psychologist: What is the effect of repetition of the mantra?

Baba: The wandering nature of the mind is controlled through the repetition of the mantra. The inherent power of the mantra also causes a subtle reaction in the subconscious. For instance, take the mundane mantra "apple." If I utter the word "apple," the image of an apple is created in your mind. Now let us consider an undesirable or negative type of word, such as "fool." If this word is directed toward someone, it will produce a powerful reaction in him; he will get very angry and upset. This is the effect and power of that word. Now take a mantra such as *Om Namah Shivaya,* which is also very powerful but which can produce a positive effect in you and allow you to feel the oneness of your being with the supreme Consciousness. Its power is such that it can catalyze an experience of your own inner Consciousness. Through continuous practice, every pore and cell of the body becomes permeated by the mantra. The mantra has so much power that it creates a sort of inner explosion that activates one's inner spiritual energy, or Kundalini Shakti. Once this inner energy is activated, it never leaves a person; it continues to aid him in his evolution until he attains spiritual perfection.

Do psychologists and psychiatrists acknowledge this inner Consciousness, the source of great joy and love, which is experienced when the mind is drawn within?

Psychologist: Some of them do, but not very many.

Baba: There is more and more interest in consciousness today. It is the duty of psychologists and psychiatrists to experience that inner Consciousness. Then they can effectively treat people who are mentally afflicted.

Psychologist: Do you mean the Consciousness beyond the mind?

Baba: Of course it is beyond the mind, but at the same time it is connected with the mind. The space of love is in the heart and also in the spiritual center in the top of the head. Once the mind touches that space, it becomes attracted to it and wants to dwell there all the time. It is said that there is no such thing as the mind, that it is not a separate entity; it is in truth a throb, or a ray, of supreme Consciousness. That supreme Consciousness is pure love, but when it gradually contracts itself and comes into contact with the different objects of the outer world, it is called the mind. And when it returns to its original form— through meditation—it becomes Consciousness once again. Therefore, we should always keep the mind in a happy condition; and for that we must practice a little *japa,* or mantra repetition, and some meditation.

Bill Link, an independent writer from the University of California, Berkeley, came to interview Muktananda on the subject of mantra for Coast Magazine.

Bill Link: What exactly is a spiritual mantra?

Baba: Mantra is the supreme Lord Himself, the supreme principle.

BL: Is mantra a vibration?

Baba: It is energy, or Shakti. When we repeat a mantra for a considerable length of time, we accumulate energy, which in turn makes the mantra more and more powerful. When this mantra is transmitted to someone else, it usually creates an immediate effect on the person who receives it because of its accumulated power. When we dwell constantly on any thought, eventually our entire being will become permeated with that thought, and mantra is the most potent kind of thought.

BL: Would you say that the person who repeats the mantra eventually becomes one with God?

Baba: There is no doubt about it. The secret of mantra is very great. By the strength of mantra we can change the entire body. The body is not an ordinary object; it can be literally transformed by a sustained act of will. We can actually convert the body into the form of the mantra.

BL: Are the subtle bodies made of energy?

Baba: All the bodies are made of certain principles. Some of these principles are physical and some are subtle. This physical body is made up of five elements, the subtle body contains seventeen principles, the causal body is made of one principle, and the supracausal body is completely pure—it transcends all principles. We experience two of these bodies in the waking and dreaming states, and sometimes we experience the third body in the deep-sleep state, but we never experience the fourth one. The fourth body can be experienced only through meditation and only after receiving the grace of a Master.

BL: You say that the causal body is made of only one element; is this element also contained in the gross, physical body?

Baba: Yes, because the physical body emanates from that single principle; that is why the third body is called the "causal" body.

BL: Do spirits, angels, and other such beings have these same bodies?

Baba: The bodies of celestial beings are made of the same elements as our second and third bodies. Some of the heavenly spirits are made of the causal material, and the lower spirits are made of the astral, or subtle elements.

BL: Can an enlightened being perceive all of his bodies?

Baba: Yes, all four bodies are seen in the process of meditation.

BL: Could you give a bit more detail about what is achieved through the use of a spiritual mantra?

Baba: First of all, a mantra removes the grossness or dullness from the intellect through which one perceives the supreme Truth. The mantra permeates the intellect and purifies it. In fact, it removes all impurities within one's entire being and thus purifies all the inner instruments. Furthermore, if you keep repeating the mantra, it eventually awakens the dormant power of the inner Self. When the Shakti is awakened, one begins to cross over the great barrier—the ocean of transmigration. This awakening is the starting point of Siddha Yoga.

BL: Are there also bad mantras?

Baba: There are certain types of mantras used just for controlling lower spirits, but we don't attach much importance to them. We attach importance to the kind of mantra that enables us to understand the truth and become one with the ultimate reality.

BL: Why does the mantra descend through the subtle bodies?

Baba: The source, the origin of the mantra lies at the most subtle level of our being, and the mantra has to return there, by descending through the different bodies, to reveal its mystery. First it purifies the physical body and then it enters into the subtle body. After purifying the subtle body, it performs the same funtion in the causal body. Then it enters into the supracausal body, at which time it converts one's entire being into the mantra—one becomes the form of the mantra.

BL: It even changes the stuff of the physical body?

Baba: Yes, each and every cell is penetrated by the mantra; each and every hair of the body becomes filled with the power of the mantra.

BL: Do you believe in astrology, and if so, do you feel that the planets affect people?

Baba: The science of astrology is a true science. According to the movements of the planets, certain effects are produced that primarily affect the events of our lives; but they also have an effect on our chakras. For example, when the planet Jupiter—the planet of the Guru—becomes influential, its effect is strong enough to touch all the chakras.

BL: When a person is born, his planets are aligned in a certain pattern. Is there any way one can change the aspect of his planets for the better?

Baba: One can change the planetary influence through *sadhana* or spiritual practice. That is the only way.

BL: Are there chants or mantras used for that?

Baba: Through chanting or *japa,* repetition of a mantra, one can accomplish anything. Chanting has tremendous power. That is why we do a lot of chanting in all our programs.

Q: How does one find the right mantra?

Baba: The mantra you receive from one who is fully realized is the right mantra. If you receive your mantra from one who has himself received something from it, you can also receive something from that mantra. There is a saying in Sanskrit: *mantra chaitanya vignata—* "Receive mantra from one who has realized its full conscious power." So if you receive a mantra from one for whom that mantra has become fully alive, fully conscious, that same mantra will also bear full fruit for you.

In ordinary life, every kind of word has an effect, and there should be no doubt about the effect of a mantra. Letters combine to form words, words combine to form sentences, and then through sentences express our meaning. That is how mantras also come into being. The mystery of mantra is profound, and from a certain viewpoint every letter is a mantra. Each word is bound to do its work, depending on what it denotes. If you ask someone to bring you water, he will bring you water; so the word "water" gets you the object water. This is a mundane mantra, and it makes its impact in your worldly life. If you go to a bakery and ask for bread, you will get bread, not something else. These mantras bring results immediately. Likewise, the *maha-mantra*, the great mantra, directs you toward the highest goal of man. By repeating the mantra, we achieve the true goal of life. According to the scriptures, it is the supreme principle which has manifested itself as mantra.

Q: You have given me the *Om Namah Shivaya* mantra, which I have been using for *japa* during the day. I have been using *Guru Om* in meditation. Is there a difference between the two mantras?

Baba: First we must understand who the Guru is. The Guru is Shiva, the universal teacher. A sage has sung a hymn to Him, saying, "I bow to Thee, O universal teacher, because from You have come all other Gurus. You are the Guru of Gurus." It is from Shiva that the line of Siddha Gurus originates. Shiva passed the mantra *Guru Om* to a being who then passed it to his successor, who in turn passed it to his successor, until it eventually came to Nityananda and then to Muktananda. That is the origin of *Guru Om,* which is the same as *Om Namah Shivaya.* It is a conscious, live mantra because it has passed through a line of Gurus.

In the scriptures, there is the story of a sage, Sanandana, who was a great worshiper of *Om Namah Shivaya.* In fact, he was exclusively devoted to this mantra and repeated it all the time. If he saw anyone, he would say *Om Namah Shivava;* if he heard anything, he would utter *Om Namah Shivaya.* He was completely immersed in *Om Namah Shivaya.* After he died, as his spirit was being taken toward heaven, he heard cries coming from a different world. He asked the heavenly messengers, "Where are those cries coming from?"

They replied, "Hell."

Sanandana said, "Why don't you take me there?"

They said, "Those who go to hell have repeated a different mantra. The mantra that you have been repeating does not merit you hell."

"I must visit there," he insisted, so the heavenly messengers took him there. When he saw so many creatures suffering the agony of hell, his heart was moved with compassion, and he began to utter *Om Namah Shivaya, Om Namah Shivaya, Om Namah Shivaya.* The scriptures say that the force of his *japa* cleansed and purified all the creatures in hell and that they were all taken to heaven along with him. This is the power of *Om Namah Shivaya.*

I'll tell you another story about the power of *Om Namah Shivaya,* which is also in the scriptures. According to Hindu mythology, when Brahma, the creator, had to create the universe, he thought about how he could best do it. He thought and thought and thought. He could not find an answer to the question until he got into a state in which he could no longer think. He began to pray, and from pure space he heard a mantra vibrating: *Om Namah Shivaya, Om Namah Shivaya, Om Nama Shivaya.* It was with the strength and power he obtained from *Om Namah Shivaya* that he made his universe.

We repeat a mantra every day that begins with, *Om namah shivaya gurave, sat-chit-ananda murtaye. Om namah shivaya* means "I bow to Shiva." Who is Shiva? Shiva is the Guru. And what is His form? It is *sat-chit-ananda,* pure being, pure consciousness, and pure bliss. The mantra continues with *nishprapanchaya,* which means "He is without any phenomenal consciousness, He lives in a state of perpetual stillness"; *shantaya,* "He is full of bliss"; *niralambaya,* "He does not depend on any factor outside of Himself"; and *tejase,* "He is pure light." *Guru Om* means the same as *Om Namah Shivaya* because Guru is Shiva and Shiva is Guru. There is no difference between the two.

What more should a person do in whose heart *Om Nama Shivaya* throbs constantly? He does not need to do any other austerities; he does not need to observe fasts or vows, go on pilgrimages, or do any other spiritual practices. Anyone can repeat this mantra, regardless of whether one is a child or an adult, whether one is a man or a woman, whether one is highly evolved or fallen, whether one is the lowest of the low or the highest of the high. This mantra suits all equally.

Om Namah Shivaya will work for everything. If your repeat *Om Namah Shivaya* eleven times, your entire day will be spent happily.

If you repeat this mantra while going to sleep, the *japa* will continue during sleep, and you will get deep sleep. If while bathing you repeat *Om Namah Shivaya*, it will be the same as taking a dip in the holy Ganges. While eating food, if you blow *Om Namah Shivaya* onto it, the food will be cleansed of all sin. If while cooking your food you repeat *Om Namah Shivaya*, the food will become so strongly charged with the power of Shakti that whoever eats it will experience Shakti. While a mother is feeding her baby, if she repeats *Om Namah Shivaya* all the time, her child will grow into a very great adult. If this mantra is repeated while doing all activities, then all these activities will become sacred rituals. While eating, repeat *Om Namah Shivaya;* while drinking, *Om Namah Shivaya;* while stepping into your car, *Om Namah Shivaya;* while driving, *Om Namah Shivaya,* but don't let go of your steering wheel while repeating the mantra!

Q: You give out three mantras: *Om Namah Shivaya, Guru Om,* and *So'ham.* I was wondering whether it makes any difference when we use them and whether we should use them alternately or stick with one for a while? Does it make any difference how we use them?

Baba: Stick to whichever mantra takes root in you, and repeat that one all the time. The goal of all the mantras is the same—they all lead you to *Om. So'ham, Guru Om,* and *Om Namah Shivaya* are all the same. If you like *So'ham* most, do *So'ham;* it is a great mantra. That is the mantra which the Siddhas give. Though the goal of the mantras is the same, one should repeat the mantra which most suits his individual temperament and level of evolution. One who is highly evolved becomes worthy of *So'ham. So'ham* brings the highest realization, but one must be worthy of it. If one is not, then one repeats *Guru Om* to become worthy of it. But the two are one.

The main thing is the goal of the mantra. *Guru Om* and *Om Namah Shivaya* are the same because Shiva is the supreme Guru. In the end, one becomes absorbed in *So'ham. So'ham* is going on all the time within.

When consciousness enters the fetus in the mother's womb in the seventh month of pregnancy, the fetus becomes aware of its own reality. Inside the womb, it looks around and is filled with tremendous sorrow. Women know what agony they undergo when the fetus begins to move in the womb. I have studied the *Garbha Upanishad,* which deals with this subject, and I also know from my medical experience that when the fetus begins to move it causes a great deal of pain to the mother and to itself. When it moves close to the digestive fire, it gets roasted. When it moves to one side, it is greeted by the stench of urine in the kidneys and bladder. When it moves to the other side it is greeted by the stench of shit in the intestines. It experiences excruciating pain. God takes pity on the fetus, and He gives it the mantra *So'ham:* "I am That." The fetus then becomes still and stays still for about two months. But when it is born, it forgets *So'ham* and begins to repeat: *Ko'ham, Ko'ham*—"Who am I? Who am I?" It loses Self-awareness. If his future is favorable, he might find a Guru at some time and receive the *So'ham* mantra, and again his awareness will be turned within.

Kabir says that *So'ham* is *ajapa japa*, the mantra that goes on within automatically. Repeat it. You will go beyond sin and virtue. This mantra is going on inside all the time; one has only to focus one's awareness on it. If you became aware of this *japa*, this natural automatic *japa*, you would see that it governs your respiratory rhythm. The scriptures say that *So'ham* vibrates within everyone. Breath comes in as *"so"* and goes out as *"ham."* If you became still and just watched the breath, you would be able to hear *So'ham*, and that would make you completely calm.

Q: After a Guru has passed away, does the mantra continue to have his power?

Baba: If he is a Siddha Guru, a perfect Guru, the mantra will continue to work with the same force. It also depends on whether the mantra is a conscious mantra or a dead mantra. A conscious mantra is one that the Guru has practiced for a long time and whose full power he has realized. That mantra has awakened his own inner Shakti and unfolded it fully and made him experience the goal of the mantra. If you receive that kind of mantra from a Guru, it will awaken your Shakti because it is a living mantra. But a mantra that one just finds in a book or hears from someone else will be a dead mantra, and it won't work.

I have met many people in America who tell me that twenty-five different people got twenty-five different *bija* mantras from the same teacher. How long must he have lived in order to have realized the full power of all twenty-five mantras! In India, most saints have achieved the highest realization with just one mantra. Just one mantra took them to heaven. *Rama-Krishna Hare* was practiced by Tukaram, *Hari Om Tat Sat* by Jnaneshwar, *Sri Ram Jai Ram* by Ramdas. Kabir was totally redeemed by *Ram, Ram, Ram,* and Tulsidas by *Sri Ram.*

It is also true that a real Guru never passes away; he is always alive. Nityananda is still alive, and he still guides me; that is why I burn a candle before his picture.

Q: Since mantra initiation usually involves some sort of special ritual performed between the Guru and the disciple, why do you simply give out a card with the mantra printed on it?

Baba: More important than any ritual is the faith of the person who receives the mantra. One with faith can receive a Siddha's mantra in any place, at any time, under any circumstances, and that mantra is guaranteed to bear its fruit. A Siddha's mantra is not inert—it's fully conscious and not bound by time, space, or ritual. Through the Siddha's grace, it bears fruit immediately. Ordinarily, there is a ritual for mantra initiation, but the main ritual is faith. Where there is no faith, ritual becomes pointless; where there is great faith, ritual becomes unnecessary.

5
INVESTIGATING
THE INNER WORLDS

Modern Western scientists have made remarkable progress in technological research. Every day, increasingly more sophisticated instruments and computers are developed which facilitate our understanding of the nature of the universe. At the same time, however, many scientists admit that their instruments are limited when it comes to investigating the nature of human consciousness. Scientific methods can take us only so far. But where the scientist's work ends, the yogi's begins. Through constant meditation, a yogi's psychic instruments—his mind, intellect, and powers of discrimination—and his subtle senses become so refined that he does not have to rely on machines and computers to collect and analyze data. The yogi becomes his own scientific instrument for the exploration of consciousness.

To a scientist or a parapsychologist who is attempting to understand supranormal phenomena through scientific methods, a Siddha Yogi (one who has traversed all levels of consciousness and who has totally mastered all physical and psychic senses) presents a rich source of information. A Siddha dwells in the state of *turiya*, the transcendental state—which is far beyond the play of phenomenal activity. He sees all phenomena as emanating from the one supreme Consciousness with which he is united. Therefore, his senses know no limitation, and he need not enlist the aid of anyone or anything outside of himself to perform his "research." What the Kirlian photographer or the bio-feedback scientist seeks to detect through sensitive instruments, the perfected yogi perceives without effort. The secrets of the universe are within his grasp; his knowledge is complete.

The scientists and researchers who come to meet Swami Muktananda express a desire to investigate phenomena that they have not yet been able to detect with their instruments. One scientist, Dr. Osis, from the American Society of Psychic Research came to visit Muktananda in New York. During their first meeting in 1970, the scientist talked about the experiments his group was conducting to test the scientific validity of spiritual phenomena. When Dr. Osis came again in 1974, he asked if Baba would come to their laboratory and demonstrate "something" for the researchers, claiming, "It would be very helpful in convincing the West about the validity of spiritual experiences."

Baba was highly amused, and laughingly told Dr. Osis, "You people have after me for four years to come to your laboratory, but you have never come to my laboratory."

In Piedmont, a parapsychologist came with his wife and asked Baba, "What is your message for scientists?"

He replied, "They should have the actual experience of their own inner Consciousness. In fact, right now three scientists are sitting in *my* laboratory." (An hour earlier, three men had come to request initiation into meditation. Baba had given them the mantra, touched each upon the forehead, and then had taken them to sit in his own bedroom.) Hearing this, the parapsychologist and his wife also asked to receive initiation, so Baba obliged and took them both into his meditation room. Later, the initiates talked about their experiences. One man had heard the sound of the mantra resounding throughout the universe; another felt intoxicated with inner joy. All of them reported strong meditation experiences.

In Los Angeles, a Kirlian photographer came to Muktananda and asked permission to take photographs which would depict the energy emanating from his body. Baba let him photograph his feet and hands and, as the man was taking the pictures, Baba told him, "The light you see is the light of Consciousness. I see it everywhere. That same light, as a conscious force, enters people when I touch them." A few moments later, Baba told the photographer, "I am feeling a lot of energy right now, but it is not for the photographs, it is for you." He touched the man between the eyebrows, then sent him to a small meditation room nearby, where he became deeply engrossed in meditation. In the meantime, everyone went for lunch and forgot about the photographer. After lunch, Baba asked, "Did the photographer leave?" Remembering that he was still in the meditation room, someone went up, awakened him and brought him down to Baba. The photographer's eyes were glowing with love and his face was flushed as he told Baba, "I had very good experiences! I saw different colored lights!"

Baba laughed and said, "Why didn't you take photographs of what you experienced?"

Baba Muktananda's conversations with researchers are penetrating. He talks from the depth of his subtle perceptions and from the vast store of his personal experiences.

During his visit to the moon, astronaut Captain Edgar Mitchell had a powerful spiritual experience. Some time later, he founded the Institute of Noetic Sciences in order to conduct research into psychic phenomena and consciousness. He came to discuss the subject with Swami Muktananda in Piedmont.

Baba: The moon is one of the great dieties of spirituality; it is the diety of the mind, and it is a giver of great peace. Your visit to the moon must have had a profound effect on your mind.

Edgar Mitchell: The moon is a very awesome object, but what seemed to have the greatest effect on me during my visit there was the view of the Earth from that vantage point.

Baba: What was the effect of that spectacle?

EM: I think it could best be described as glimpses of cosmic consciousness, identification with universal processes—for approximately thirty hours, an experience of unity between myself and the universal processes.

Baba: That's very good. You know, it is quite possible to see the different worlds of the cosmos—the world of the moon, Jupiter, heaven, and hell (these, too, are real worlds)—and it is possible to see them distinctly through the grace of the inner energy, as clearly as you saw the moon when you were there. For instance, if you moved this radio dial less than an inch, you could tune in to countries on different sides of the world; America is only half an inch away from India as far as this instrument is concerned. Likewise, inside, all the different worlds are very, very close once you gain access to the inner space. If you tried to visit these worlds in your physical body, in your ordinary waking state, you would find them very far away, but if you visited these same worlds through the inner space by means of the supracausal body—the fourth body—these worlds would become very close.

EM: I think I have personally experienced such traveling—under uncontrolled conditions—but it has happened to me occasionally. My main concern now, after having had such travel experiences, both external and internal, is to somehow try to bring together the best ideas and notions of the Western scientific world and those of the mystical, metaphysical worlds into a body of common knowledge. My quest, at this point, is to try to build a body of knowledge that represents a marriage of these two ways of thought.

Baba: The fact is that scientific knowledge and spiritual knowledge are already married.

EM: Except that people don't recognize it.

Baba: People don't recognize even their own reality. The truth is that the outer and inner, the mundane and spiritual, are really one.

EM: I am convinced that in our Western way of thinking we have blinded ourselves to the fact that it is truly one universe and that it is only our perspective that keeps the scientific and the spiritual apart.

Baba: Today, more and more people are studying consciousness, but they still don't seem to be aware that it is the subtle energy of the divine Consciousness which has become the physical universe.

EM: I think that they will before very long. The problem is the current scientific concept that matter rather than consciousness is the primordial stuff. When that thinking changes, the entire scientific body of truth will change, and I feel that this change is only a few years away.

Baba: Once man begins to understand Consciousness he will begin to understand the true nature of things. After people like you return from different planets, they will come up with fresh observations and insights, which will speed up man's progress in this field. Recently, I have met many psychologists—some of them quite well known and distinguished—and in my talks with them, I saw that many of them are aware of the fact that Consciousness is everything, but they don't have the direct, personal experience of it.

EM: What we are seeing is the intellectual acceptance that our previous notions were wrong, and science is beginning to realize the necessity for studying consciousness. The difficulty is the Western scientific notion that the scientist must never let his feelings be a part of his experiment. Because of this, the scientist never permits himself to seek an experience of his own mind—his own consciousness. When scientists begin pursuing such an experience, their awareness of things will surely change.

Baba: It is necessary for scientists to experience their own reality through meditation. Once we experience inner truth directly through meditation, it becomes easy for us to perceive Truth in the outer world and to understand nature's secrets and mysteries.

EM: My immediate concern is in leading scientists to accept the fact that the mind is not at all what it is understood to be by modern science. And although we are beginning to realize that the study of psychic phenomena is a barren endeavor, at least it has been of value in demonstrating to Western scientists that their notion of reality is incorrect and they must look further.

Baba: If demonstrating the validity of these psychic phenomena could help this cause, it would be a very creative step.

EM: I agree, but the study of psychic phenomena is difficult to conduct scientifically when one has to deal mainly with people whose psychic talents are undisciplined and erratic. We have many natural psychics readily available for study, but unfortunately they seldom demonstrate any spirituality.

Baba: Your problem is understandable. The spiritual Masters who come from established traditions, or lineages, have so far indicated that it is against their etiquette to demonstrate such powers, but perhaps you will find some who will be willing to. In India, the spiritual Masters look upon the display of psychic powers with tremendous disdain. Once, when my Guru was alive, I attempted something of that sort, and he came after me with a big club in his hand.

EM: I completely understand and agree with the need for such a position among spiritual Masters. While we are on the subject of psychic powers, I would like to ask you a question concerning the large number of mostly ordinary people in our culture—and, perhaps, yours as well—who exhibit some extraordinary psychic ability. Most of these people have obviously not attained such power through spiritual practices—they seem to have acquired their gifts naturally—and I want to know why these abilities seem to spring up in some people without any apparent reason.

Baba: There is an explanation for this in our tradition. To illustrate it for you, I need only point out the large number of people who are engaged in spiritual pursuits around me. Now, it is quite likely that many of them may not become realized before they end this lifetime, in which case, when they again take birth, whatever effort they have performed in this life will certainly not be lost to them. In their next life, they will exhibit certain unusual powers, right from birth—powers such as clairvoyance, clairaudience, and so on. Such powers do not come to a person haphazardly; they are the result of practice done in a past life.

EM: I would also like to ask your opinion in another matter. I come in contact with a great many people with psychic ability, and I am interested in finding a good method of getting these people to recognize that they have a unique talent and that it is especially important for them to work on their own spiritual well-being. It is of great concern to me that such people be urged to develop in the spiritual direction.

Baba: It seems to me that, if things were put to them in a certain manner, they would be able to grasp the importance of this very quickly. For example, if you talked to them about Kundalini Shakti, about the source of their powers, they would become interested in looking into such things. You could confront them with questions such as, "What is the source of these powers that you have?" or "Who is the one inside you from whom you get all this information?" Not long ago, a couple of psychics—very genuine people—came here. Later, one of them returned and told me that after she had received my touch she opened up in a completely different way, and she now realized that what she had been doing before was relatively insignificant—that all her previous psychic readings had been nothing compared to what had begun happening to her as a result of the inner awakening of the Kundalini Shakti. She said that she now realized that in spite of all her psychic readings she had been far, far away from the Truth.

EM: That's very encouraging. I'm becoming more and more concerned with the dangers of our society becoming preoccupied with psychic events, and I feel it is essential that this interest be redirected into more spiritual areas.

Baba: I feel that many would quite easily be drawn to the spiritual path if people such as you talked to them about psychic phenomena from a spiritual point of view.

EM: We are trying to do that, but are handicapped by the fact that, because of modern scientific materialism, religious traditions have pretty much been rejected in this country. Maybe it is good that some outmoded traditions give way, but to direct people now toward true spirituality is not easy. Our scientific approach has tended to discredit the religious approach in this country.

Baba: What you say is true. Still, the more you talk to people about your own inner experiences and the more friendly contacts you establish with the scientific community, the easier it will be for you to get them to accept what you have to tell them. I also understand that you have expressed the belief—have you not?—that, if some of the spiritual phenomena could be detected by physical instruments, scientists would accept the testimony of those instruments.

EM: Yes, that is exactly what we are trying to accomplish, but progress is very slow.

Baba: Unfortunately, the inner phenomena are so subtle that I wonder whether they can ever be captured by even the most refined instruments. For instance, there is a most extraordinary effulgence in the *sahasrara*—the spiritual center in the crown of the head. This light contains a tinge of gold and a tinge of blue, and many people have experienced it blazing there. Right in the center of this light is a dot, which we call the Blue Pearl. This dot comes out of the eyes and stands before you in meditation, as though it were a concrete physical object. Then it returns through the eyes to its abode inside the cerebral center, and it is so subtle that the eyes do not even feel its passage. Now, I wonder if any instrument, no matter how sophisticated, could ever record that?

EM: That is the question that troubles us because we know that these things are extremely subtle. Perhaps through meditation we can gain insights into how to build such physical instruments. I am afraid that we won't be able to develop anything delicate enough to be able to detect phenomena such as those you have described, but we will keep trying, and someday maybe we'll succeed.

Baba: I congratulate you on your determination. I am sure that, if you continue as you are doing, you may well come up with something soon. In reality, Consciousness has become matter and matter is only Consciousness, and there was a time when the two were one. A mirror reflects a face; the face is a material object and so is the mirror, but the image of the face in the mirror is a subtle object. Perhaps you may be able to evolve some kind of an instrument that, like a mirror, will reflect an object as subtle as the inner Self. Occasionally I put on very thick glasses just for the sake of an experiment, and the Blue Pearl emerges from within, piercing the thick glass without breaking it.

EM: May I ask more about your vision of the Blue Pearl? You think you see it with your physical eyes. If you put a mirror in front of yourself at that time, would you see the Pearl's reflection in the mirror, as well as directly?

Baba: Unfortunately, I can't keep a mirror in front of me constantly. You see, the Blue Pearl is supremely free, and it alone decides when it will emerge, how long it will stay, and when it will come back. Sometimes it does not appear for a long while, and at other times it reveals itself quite frequently. The Blue Pearl is its own master. There is tremendous magic in it. It is the Blue Pearl which serves as the vehicle for astral travel. This Blue Pearl is the inner Self, and that is what all the great Masters of India have said.

EM: The crucial point in getting scientists to understand these concepts is describing the conscious energy that we are dealing with in spiritual phenomena in terms of matter or its relationship with matter. As you said earlier, Consciousness and matter are interchangeable, and, in the beginning, everything was Consciousness. But the process through which Consciousness becomes matter and the relationship between energy and Consciousness are the things that we somehow must explain. I have experienced it, you experience it all the time, and anyone else can experience it too, using the discipline that you teach; but it must be understood and explained in scientific terms before instruments can be built to detect such subtle phenomena.

Baba: Perhaps you will find a way, but it won't be easy to detect such things with physical instruments. I pursued my spiritual discipline for a long time after receiving grace from my Guru, who was a fully realized Master, and it was only after a long period of practice that I had the experience of the Blue Pearl. Even now it is not under my direct control. Though the Blue Pearl looks infinitesimal, it contains the entire cosmos; it is the most magical thing in existence.

EM: Can you explain to me its nature or purpose? How does the Blue Pearl relate to the soul, or the essence of human consciousness?

Baba: The Blue Pearl is the essence itself. Its nature is bliss; it is the giver of peace. When I say it is a pearl, you shouldn't think that it is some kind of concrete object; "pearl" doesn't mean that it is something material. The Blue Pearl is the essence of the inner Self, and it is experienced only when one reaches the fourth and highest state of consciousness.

EM: You seem to be describing a perceptual reality of a particular state of consciousness.

Baba: Beyond the Blue Pearl lies the pure Being, who has been described as being "without attribute, quality, or form." After one has had an experience of the Blue Pearl, there comes a time when the Blue Pearl explodes, and its light is scattered throughout the cosmos. Then it becomes possible to see even with the physical eyes the Blue Pearl shimmering everywhere. The entire cosmos becomes engulfed in blue light. When you boil water in a kettle, you can watch the vapor rise from it, and the blue, misty light of Consciousness appears just like that, shimmering everywhere, because that's what everything is made of. I wonder how such a thing could be detected by instruments?

EM: I would suspect that the energy you are describing is far more subtle than some other energies that we have yet to understand. We will probably have to understand those less subtle energies first and then just keep refining our understanding until someday we will perhaps reach an understanding of the energy you describe.

Baba: That is true. There are four bodies, one within the other, and we perceive them through meditation. These four bodies represent the four planes of reality—physical, subtle, causal, and supra-causal—and as one passes from one plane to another, new vistas are revealed, new worlds are opened up.

Developing instruments to record such phenomena may answer a certain need, but the important thing is to experience them personally, and instruments can never give you that experience. If scientists could detect the Blue Pearl with instruments, they would accept its existence and spend years and years thinking about it, talking about it, and writing down theories about it; but it is much more important to actually meditate for a while, to go within and experience the Blue Pearl for yourself because the experience will completely transform you. You will experience inner bliss, you will be able to see distant objects and hear distant sounds, and you will be filled with celestial music. From the inner firmament nectar will drip, and as you taste this nectar you will be overwhelmed with ecstasy. This experience is the most exciting one available to man, and when you have it, you realize how delicious life can be.

EM: I understand and believe that, but I feel that an objective, scientific measurement would at least serve to bring agreement among researchers as far as terminology is concerned. For example, students of Muktananda are looking for the Blue Pearl, whereas the students of another Guru may describe it as a white pearl, and for years and years into the future, devotees will argue over whether it is blue or white—they will spend all their time arguing about the color rather than experiencing the essence. That is why I think it is better to describe it, if possible, in terms that we can agree upon by objective measurement. If we rely mainly on personal observations, our descriptions may differ because we are trying to describe a subjective reality that each of us might perceive differently.

Baba: Yes, that's all right if you can do it, but the Blue Pearl has a definite color, and that is blue. That cannot change. For instance, I look at you and your shirt is white, and that can't change; it can't be different for two people. You will find testimony about the color of the Blue Pearl in the writings of many great Siddhas—great Masters—and you will find that they have all described it the same way.

EM: That is also an important kind of evidence. If independent observers describe it in the same way, without interaction with each other, we can accept that as a reasonably good guide in determining what anyone else would see.

Baba: That is the absolute truth.

EM: Of course, another problem is the one of language. Compared with Sanskrit, our Western languages have very few terms that describe internal states.

Baba: At my Ashram, I have had professors of languages such as French, Spanish, and Italian engaged in translating my books, and they say that it is often very difficult to find adequate words in their languages.

EM: I have taken a great deal of your time.

Baba: I am very happy that you have come, and I am proud of you because, in this very body, you have traveled to the moon and back. The difference between you and me is that while you went to the moon in the physical body I traveled there in the subtle body.

EM: Your journey must have cost a lot less money than mine.

Baba: And much less effort, too; things are easier if you have the grace of the Blue Pearl working for you. It is my sincere hope that one day scientists will be able to capture it with instruments.

EM: I hope so too, but even if we aren't able to do that, at least we still have enlightened beings such as you to guide us.

Baba: Yes, such beings can transmit experience to thousands—the experience of supreme truth.

EM: I am anxious to have another meeting.

Baba: I hope that we will meet again and again until you have an experience of the Blue Pearl.

Soon after his arrival in California, Baba Muktananda was invited to speak at Stanford University. Prior to his lecture, a reception was held where he was introduced to many Stanford professors. Dr. William Tiller, a professor of physics, was at that reception and came to see Muktananda again in Piedmont.

Dr. Tiller: When I met you, I felt as if we were old friends.

Baba: One who is in contact with the inner Self is an old friend of everyone.

WT: I am trying to develop a rigorous science of the nonphysical universe, but the territory is so vast and the map is so big that I hardly know where to begin. One must go where humanity is and cast it in that language. How does one begin to unravel the picture and communicate it?

Baba: You have to go back to the origin of the five elements, which is described in the Upanishads. According to the Upanishads, which have given an account of creation, everything has come from the same source, called pure Being. From pure Being emerges pure space. When pure space begins to vibrate, air, the next element, comes into being. From the friction of air comes fire, and fire then produces water in the same way that we begin to sweat when it is hot. And when the sediment from water settles the element of earth arises. You must study these physical elements in all their different manifestations. For example, the earth produces the food that man eats to sustain his life. From food, the sexual fluid is generated. And from the sexual fluid, the human body is formed. A drop of sexual fluid is therefore really nothing but earth. So the human body also originates from the same source, pure Being. I have given you the basic outline; it has been elaborated upon in vast philosophical works.

You should then study the human body and learn how it is composed of the five elements. The human body is a microcosm; the universe is the macrocosm. Whatever you find in the universe, you will also find in the body. Whatever is solid in the body, such as bone, is derived from the earth principle. All the bodily fluids, such as semen and blood, come from the water principle. The body derives its individual prana, or life force, from the universal, cosmic prana; the two are actually one according to the Upanishads.

But even after studying this philosophy, you will have to meditate to realize its validity.

WT: The best way to describe the work I have done so far is to use the poetic analogy of peeling off the layers of an onion. At the first layer, one is confronted by the need to study the human body. Getting through the second layer means working meaningfully and quantitatively with subtle energies, describing them with the same thoroughness with which we have already described electromagnetic energies and things of this nature. That's where I am now, and I am asking about that level.

Baba: This analogy of an onion is also used in our philosophical works. There are two levels of research: the physical and the subtle. Modern science is engaged in research on the physical level. All that you have done so far is quite valid. But for research on the subtle level, we have to turn to meditation, through which we can study the subtle planes directly. That is possible only through an awakened Kundalini.

WT: I certainly agree with that. The problem that I face is how to use meditation to describe the subtle energies with as much precision as our descriptions of the physical energies.

Baba: Yes, it may be a problem, but at the same time we must remember that what you call electromagnetic energy is gross in comparison with the Kundalini. Through my own inner research, I have discovered this energy, which is so powerful that, if I gave you just a touch, it would feel like an electric shock. Though I look like anybody else on the outside, through Kundalini awakening my inner body has been thrown into a kind of furnace, and there it has become completely purged of impurities and regenerated.

Just as you have physical instruments to investigate physical phenomena, we yogis have subtle instruments, which are even more effective than physical instruments. For instance, though my eyes look like anybody else's, they have become refined by that subtle energy active within me. My ears, nose, and mental energies have also become refined, as have the inner psychic instruments—ego, mind, unconscious mind, and intellect.

My physical eyes have become so refined and pure that I can see a bluish light pervading everywhere, which not even your most sophisticated instruments can see. That light is just like the delicate after-image that persists when a flash-bulb goes off. That bluish light keeps sparkling all the time, everywhere. At this very moment, I can see it within you and all around us; it's there in the wall, it's there in pure space—it's everywhere. It's so fascinatingly beautiful that, as one watches it, one is enraptured. This light is not like a continuous glow; it's made up of particles like tiny sparks.

Also, there is a blue dot, called the Blue Pearl, in the crown of the head, which is luminous like radium. If you want to investigate the phenomena I am talking about, you will have to take the help of this Blue Pearl. Once you see this Pearl, it bestows tremendous energy and new power to your body and mind—to your whole organism—and by means of that you can perceive and understand anything.

WT: Is it important to determine the position of the Pearl, say, at the pineal gland or the crown chakra?

Baba: The Blue Pearl is situated in the middle of the cerebral center. If I turn my vision upward, even now, I can see it right in the middle of the cerebrum. Sometimes it emerges from my eye and stands in front of me. Yogis worship the Blue Pearl with great devotion, as a deity. If we remember it all the time with love, it reveals its beauty to us. Now, as I am talking to you, it may at any moment come out like a flash. Although yogis have complete control over the body, they don't have any control over the Blue Pearl. However, one can acquire the ability to see it over and over again. Compared to the bliss of this vision, what we normally consider as pleasurable—eating, drinking, or smoking—totally fades into insignificance and is no longer pleasurable.

WT: I agree.

Baba: I am not simply repeating what is written in books; I am speaking from my direct observation, and I have described these things systematically and at length in my book, *Play of Consciousness.* Most saints keep all these details very secret, but I have been compelled to disclose them to the whole world.

This Blue Pearl has endless resources and power. Whenever you want to receive a message from it, it will take on the form of your Guru and give you instruction. In India, people believe that the personal form of the Lord is a reality. The different divine manifestations are given names such as Rama or Krishna or Shiva. There was a time when I did not adhere to this belief in a personal divinity, but after I had the vision of the Blue Pearl and after I saw all the manifestations appearing within it, I accepted its reality.

WT: I accept its reality as well.

Baba: You won't find these descriptions in any of the traditional philosophical scriptures, because the ancient saints didn't reveal these secrets. But some of them did speak of these mysteries in veiled language in their poetry.

WT: Now seems to be the time for such things to be revealed.

Baba: I have revealed them to millions of people in India, and now I have come to America. You professors can do tremendous work if, just as you are conducting external research, you conducted internal research and wrote about that. Your word has great weight with students, as well as with the general public.

WT: That's just what I am doing.

Baba: I can see the truth of that by looking at your face and into your eyes. One way in which the Indian tradition differs from the Western tradition is that in India we rely more on the Guru. Instead of conducting research on any subject, we depend on a Guru for the attainment of full knowledge about such matters. In India, the Guru is honored very highly because we do not look upon a Guru as a human being. The Upanishads say that one who investigates the nature of God becomes God in the course of his investigation. So we honor the Guru as God, not as a human being. This glory comes to one by his direct experience of that Blue Pearl because it is the highest divine reality. This entire cosmos is like a tiny speck within that blue dot.

Before I had this illumination, I read a poem of Swami Ram Tirth, who was a distinguished professor of mathematics before he renounced the world and became a sannyasi, a monk. In that poem he writes, "The wind that blows is in me, in me, in me. The water that flows is in me, in me, in me. The sun that rises is in me, in me, in me." I used to wonder if perhaps he had gone crazy, but after my illumination I realized the total truth of his experience.

WT: I agree. It's clear that in the company of the Guru an aspirant can do and perceive things that he cannot normally accomplish on his own. Eventually, however, he *is* able to accomplish these things on his own. How does one make the transition from needing someone else's radiation to generating it within himself?

Baba: In the course of time, the disciple comes to absorb the Guru's perfection into his being, and then he radiates it. The transition takes place through constant absorption of the Guru's light and by constantly following the practices recommended by him with regularity. Look at that boy sitting on his father's lap. When he grows up, he too will become a father. Likewise, a disciple becomes a Guru. Tukaram Maharaj, a great Indian saint, said, "The Guru's glory is unfathomable." When iron comes in contact with a philosopher's stone, it becomes transmuted into gold, but it doesn't become another philosopher's stone. After a disciple comes in contact with a Guru, he will become a Guru and can operate in perfect freedom. In that state, though the disciple does not look upon himself as being in any way smaller than his Guru, his gratitude keeps him filled with love for the Guru.

WT: Yes, I understand.

Baba: Therefore, we honor the Guru very highly. The truth is that to honor the Guru is to honor your own inner Self. When we worship any form of the Lord, we should be aware that we are really worshiping our own Self in that form.

WT: I also feel that we are all part of one organism.

Baba: What I do for you, I really do for myself. The happiness that begins to vibrate in you, becomes reflected in my own heart. This is a mystery of the truth. You are a very fine person, and it has given me great delight to have had this talk with you.

Jacques Valle, an author and researcher on the subject of unidentified flying objects (UFOs) had read Play of Consciousness *and was impressed by Muktanada's descriptions of different worlds visited during meditation. Because of what he had read, Valle came to meet Baba to discuss the subject further.*

(Before Baba arrived for the interview, Mr. Valle mentioned to others present that he believes scientific data alone will not give conclusive information on the subject of UFOs. Baba was told this when he arrived, and the interview began with his response.)

Baba: It is true that only through spirituality and faith can you discover the truth about UFOs. UFOs do exist, and the inhabitants of higher realms do visit the earth. If you read Hindu mythology, you will find references to this. In modern times as well, people have seen UFOs. I know of a great Siddha being, a perfect Master, Tukaram Maharaj, who was initiated by a Guru from another, higher plane; so I believe in the existence of UFOs.

JV: You speak of higher "planes" and not of planets. Are these planes physical or spiritual?

Baba: There are higher planes that are more subtle than the physical one. *Pitruloka*, for example, is the world of ancestors; *Swargaloka* is heaven; and there is a realm called *Siddhaloka*, where great beings such as Bhagawan Nityananda, Zipruanna, and Shirdi Sai Baba live.

JV: What prevents us from having access to these planes?

Baba: They are very, very far away. Still, nothing prevents us from seeing them if we want to. Just as it's true that you can't visit San Francisco while sitting right here, neither can you visit these higher realms unless you make the proper effort to see them. However, the beings there can visit us more easily because their knowledge and strength of mind are much greater than ours.

Just as we have our different kinds of aircraft, the beings from these *lokas* have their unique vehicles, although they are not like our machines. They are propelled by the mind and go wherever their pilots will them.

One who meditates with Kundalini yoga understands these things more easily than other people. A meditator doesn't pursue such knowledge; he just meditates on his own Self. It is through this process that he becomes aware of these worlds.

You won't find our sun or moon in these higher realms; there is no day or night. You will find just light. In *Siddhaloka*, for example, there is only blue light. This is the realm of fully realized beings, and many, many of these perfect Masters live there. No being who attains this realm ever falls from that high state, but occasionally, as I mentioned earlier, one of these Masters descends to Earth temporarily to initiate a worthy seeker. These Siddhas travel faster than the speed of light or thought, and they fly in vehicles that assume whatever form the Master wills them to have.

JV: Can they also create at will the shape of their visible form?

Baba: Normally their bodies are made of substances so subtle that we cannot perceive them, but whenever those beings feel like showing a physical manifestation, they can take on any form they wish to be seen in. In order to initiate people on Earth, they have to take on a physical form; otherwise, they can't initiate them. Sometimes they even take birth in this world.

Siddhaloka is one of the farthest planes from our own. One of the nearer planes is called *Pitruloka*, the world of ancestors. In India, there is a custom performed once each year for fifteen days whereby people pay respects to their ancestors and worship them with offerings of delicious food. Even now this custom prevails, and the food offered to the ancestors during those fifteen days will feed them for an entire year, until the next fifteen-day offering.

There are many different planes where gods and goddesses live, and some Indians worship and follow austerities for quite a long time to please these gods and goddesses. When they are pleased, they grant whatever boon has been asked for. For example, a person may be granted a supernatural power. The forms of these gods and goddesses are not very different from our own. People who meditate a lot and have very high meditations see all these beings very clearly. Once you have personally seen all these different worlds, you no longer think of them as myths; you know that they exist.

In the world of Indra, which we call heaven, all the inhabitants are completely equal, and they have extremely beautiful bodies. They do not age, become ill, or die, yet eventually all the inhabitants of *Indraloka* must leave to reincarnate on Earth. A meditator is able to visit this plane when messengers of Indra come and escort him to that world, where he is then honored, particularly if he is a practitioner of Siddha Yoga. The vehicle used for this journey is the Blue Star.

These days many people believe not only in unidentified flying objects, but also that the beings who come here in those vehicles occasionally take a few Earth people with them when they go back to their realms. There is evidence to support such belief. If you read the *Mahabharata*, you will find the account of Arjuna, who visited heaven while still in his physical form.

In this universe there are many, many different planes of existence. Not only this world and this sky exist, but infinite planes of existence, and they all have different kinds of life. Some beings of the higher realms live on air; they don't need to eat bread or milk or cheese. The great beings in *Siddhaloka* live solely on light, on Consciousness, and what is a thousand years for us is only one moment to them.

This may sound fantastic, but it's absolutely true. You cannot discover the truth of this by using scientific knowledge because it goes beyond physical science. Only a yogi who meditates and has great faith can help you understand such things. With the help of such a yogi, you can understand and experience these higher planes. I know personally that these planes exist; I have met great beings from higher planes. There are three ancient abodes of Siddhas, called Siddha *pithas*, and I used to visit them a lot. One is in Tibet, another is in

Girnar, and the third is on the mountain known as Shri Sailam, where people are always chanting. I was very fond of going there; I loved to live on that mountain because it's like an ashram.

JV: People in many countries have been confronted with this sort of phenomenon, even though they were not looking for spiritual experiences. As a result, many have undergone changes in their personalities which frightened them. What advice can you give to these people?

Baba: No matter which plane you go to or which beings you meet, if you have the right understanding, these experiences will be beneficial to you. Most people who meet these beings don't understand what is happening to them, and that is why they become frightened. Instead of deriving joy, happiness, and mental peace from such experiences, they derive only unhappiness and anxiety. Such people should seek the company of saints because a saint will take charge of the situation immediately and bring them back to a normal condition.

The morning after I received Shaktipat, or divine initiation, from my Guru, my mind was very perturbed, but not long after I was made to understand exactly what was happening to me, and I felt very happy, very blessed.

These things happen when Shakti is transmitted into you. After receiving Shaktipat, you eventually become enlightened, but the beginning stages can be a little shaky, and you have to understand things very well or else you may think you are going crazy. I've come across many, many people whose Shakti was somehow awakened, and they began having such strange experiences that their parents thought them to be mentally ill and put them in the hospital. As soon as I give such people right understanding, everything is fine.

The yoga of Shaktipat is a very significant and important yoga; it is not like other, ordinary yogas. This yoga is called Siddha Yoga, and it can unfold inside you only when you receive the grace of a Siddha being.

JV: It has been a great honor to be in your presence.

Baba: You are a very nice man. You have been listening very carefully and intently. Some people come and talk about trivial things, and the time just goes by. I don't speak to them about significant things because they are not interested. But you are a very nice man, and I feel that some work of the Shakti is going on within you—the beginning of a revolution. Your eyes show what is happening within you; they are full of love.

Several biofeedback scientists came to meet Baba, hoping to have the opportunity of registering his brain waves on their machines. This conversation between Baba and one such scientist took place in New York.

Baba: What sort of research are you engaged in?

Scientist: What we do is convert brain waves to a kind of sound, like music, so a person can hear his own waves. The sound becomes like a mirror of what is happening in the subject's brain. Because the sound is a mirror, people can, by learning to manipulate the sound, learn to manipulate their brain waves as well.

Baba: That is one way; but there is another way, in which one goes within through meditation, maintaining full awareness, and then he can be aware of what is happening inside and know exactly where he is. What you detect as waves in the brain are really waves of Consciousness. The inner Self, or the Atman, is vibrating all the time, it is constantly sending out waves.

Scientist: We have found that the waves differ greatly according to the person's state of consciousness.

Baba: Can you find out from the brain waves if a person is angry or agitated? That is one state of consciousness. Then there are two other levels of awareness. One is called *savikalpa*, in which there is still some thought, so you would be able to detect brain waves. The other is *nirvikalpa* state, which is totally free from thought, and there the waves would cease. Beyond even those states is the state of *turiyatita* in which the mind ceases to exist altogether.

Scientist: Our experiments have shown that repetition of the mantra greatly affects the quality of a person's brain waves.

Baba: Even more than this, if you repeat the mantra over a long period of time, the subtle vibrations of that mantra eventually permeate all your blood corpuscles, all your vital fluids, and all the cells of your body. Furthermore, the vibrations may even pass into the shoes that you wear; if there were an instrument that could detect subtle mantra waves, it would be able to pick up the waves from the shoes of someone who practices *japa* continually.

In Dharwar, a part of India, there was a man who was being operated on, and he needed blood. The man was given the blood of a saint, and while he was recovering from the operation, the mantra that the saint practiced continually began to repeat itself automatically inside him, because the saint's blood was so charged with the mantra's vibrations. This story is the absolute truth, and it merits serious consideration. These days, if someone has diabetes or high blood pressure, a medical expert will ask him, "Did your father have this? Did you grandfather have it?" And if the patient were to ask the doctor, "Why do you want all this information?" the doctor would say, "This illness is hereditary; it is passed through the genes." So is it surprising to learn that a mantra can be inherited through blood?

In fact, what we call matter is nothing but a manifestation of Consciousness. A detecting machine is the same as that which it detects. And, in order to interpret the detector, you need a human being, don't you? You need a conscious, human brain. An instrument detects something happening inside somebody, but it is somebody's brain which has to interpret what the instrument has detected.

I'm not against instruments; I'm all for them. In the field of instrumental research, you people have made tremendous advances. All that I am saying is that the instrument itself cannot know the information it is picking up. What is really happening, then, is that the mind is using an instrument to detect something happening to itself, and the same mind then has to interpret and understand what the instrument has detected.

Scientist: My idea of the Guru is that he also acts as a mirror of other people's consciousness; in that way, the Guru is the ideal biofeedback machine.

Baba: That's true.

Scientist: It is my hope that by making a mirror of the mind we can have many gurus to help people understand themselves better.

Baba: It can certainly be of some help, but it can't be a substitute. An instrument or a machine can only serve as a mechanical guru; it can never serve as a yoga guru. Our Siddha Gurus are of a different order. If such a being were to merely touch you—here, between the eyebrows —a totally new and permanent process would be activated through which the mind begins to calm down automatically. The heart also begins to calm down, anger subsides, and the ego begins to diminish spontaneously. Until one gains total perfection, the effect of the touch keeps working all the time. Through this process, one is able to experience directly a place in the heart where a light vibrates constantly. Can that be detected by your instruments?

Scientist: No, I have not detected that.

Baba: There is also a light between the eyebrows which is like a candle flame. Can that be detected? It is not only I who have seen these things; there must be many others with me who have seen them too. There is also a great effulgence here, in the crown of the head. Its brilliance surpasses the light of a thousand suns, and it is extremely beautiful—full of tremendous delight. An instrument should also be able to detect that. The light is tinged with blue, gold, and black, and seeing it is not an hallucination. You could find quite a few people here who would be able to describe that experience to you. And in the midst of it all there is a blue jewel, which is very tiny, very agile, and supremely fascinating. Again, this is not just a figment of imagination; it actually exists.

Scientist: I would be interested in trying to detect them in Babaji.

Baba: It's fine if you want to try to detect these things in me, but it would be much better for you to receive some Shakti from me and then make the test within yourself. Would you like to do that?

At the invitation of Werner Erhard, Swami Muktananda went to Aspen, Colorado, for a special "est Presents" lecture program. Dr. John Lilly, a well-known author and researcher, attended the lecture and came with Werner the next day to meet Baba.

John Lilly: There are several scientists here who are interested in studying the phenomenon of miracles.

Baba: I'm sure it is interesting for scientists to study miracles, but there isn't anything particularly important in them. There are three types of miracles, or *siddhis*. The first is nothing more than sleight-of-hand. The second is unnatural *siddhis*, which are accomplished by mental power. And the third type occurs when a ghost or evil spirit is propitiated, who then does the work of the "miracle." All these are trivial.

Swami Vivekananda tells a story about a Brahmin who possessed miraculous powers. When Vivekananda went to meet the man in Hyderabad, he found the Brahmin suffering from a high fever. The Brahmin recognized Vivekananda as a very high being and asked the swami to touch his head. Vivekananda did so, and immediately the man's fever subsided. Vivekananda asked to see a demonstration of his powers. The Brahmin readily agreed and, after leading Vivekananda and his companions into another room, removed all his clothes except his loincloth. It was very cold, and Vivekananda put a blanket around the ailing man to prevent a recurrence of fever. The yogi told Vivekananda and his friends to write down whatever they desired on a piece of paper and give it to him. They wrote down the names of fruits that were not in season in that part of the country, such as grapes and oranges, and gave the paper to the Brahmin. In a few minutes he opened his blanket and out tumbled dozens of pieces of fruit—the same kind that had been requested. Everyone began to eat the *prasad*, and Vivekananda commented on how sweet it tasted. A few moments later the yogi produced a bunch of perfectly formed roses covered with dew. When Vivekananda asked for an explanation, the "magician" said it was just sleight-of-hand.

There are many such miracle mongers in the part of India where I live. One is called "Coconut Baba." You ask him a question and give him a coconut. He breaks open the coconut in your presence, and a piece of paper comes out with your answer written on it in red ink.

I thought we were going to talk about more important matters, but now that this subject has come up, let me tell you that I learned all these tricks too; but that was before I met my Guru. God isn't in them; so it's pointless for a saint to have anything to do with them.

Amma's younger brother and his wife went to see a lady who materialized objects such as *kumkum*, flowers, ashes, and ornaments. She gave them a gold statue of Krishna, but within three months, it tarnished and turned into brass. Somebody once showed me a watch supposedly materialized by a miracle man. I opened it from the back and had to laugh: "It looks as if even heavenly watches are marked 'Made in Switzerland'!"

There was a man who used to bother my Baba a lot. That man would be walking along and if a girl happened to laugh at him, he would make a movement with his stick and the girl's skirt would fly up by itself. He was dreadful. He would go to fairs and hang out around the candy stand, flipping up the skirts of all the girls who went by and, with another movement, making candy come flying out of the stand, landing near him. I remember seeing him do that when I was a young man. One day, a wedding was to be held by a wealthy family. The father was a great devotee of my Baba and invited him to the wedding, seating him in the place of honor. This man also happened to invite the magician, who became jealous because Baba was being treated with such respect. The magician complained, "Why have you given me such an ordinary seat? Is that sadhu as powerful as I am?" He took out a pinch of tobacco, recited some mantras over it, and offered it to Baba. People were frightened when they saw that. My Baba said, "Since you've poisoned this tobacco with your mantras, you'd better not offer it to me. I'm not concerned about what will happen to me, but why should you die?" The magician said, "Don't worry, nothing will happen to me." Baba put the tobacco in his mouth and started chewing it, and at the same moment, the magician collapsed and had to be taken to a hospital, where he died. Many people celebrated because the magician had become such a nuisance. Afterward, his followers brought a lawsuit against Baba. My Baba said, "I was the one who chewed the tobacco, but he was the one who died. What can I do about it?"

There is a text that low magicians can use to kill people, which has no other use except to cause harm. It would be all right to direct it against someone like me because I am quite *sattvic*—the trick would boomerang back to the magician and do him double the harm. Black magic has no effect on pure people. Where there is faith in the Self, where the *Gita* is recited and the *Vedas* are chanted, such tricks are powerless.

JL: Patanjali has described five sources of *siddhis*, or powers: birth, mantras, austerities, herbs, and samadhi.

Baba: Siddhis possessed at birth are the result of effort put forth in a previous lifetime. Siddhas, too, are sometimes born with full powers. My Baba, for example, was a born Siddha. Such a Master is the greatest of all; he descends directly from *Siddhaloka*. There is also a *siddhi* derived from repetition of mantra. That boy (Baba points to a boy sitting nearby) will acquire this type of *siddhi* soon because his mantra has already descended to his throat; when it descends to his heart, the *siddhi* will come to him. If one repeats a mantra properly, it descends from the tongue to the throat, from the throat to the heart, and from the heart to the navel. And then all its power is completely unlocked.

There are also the *siddhis* derived from herbs, but those are ordinary *siddhis*—they are only temporary. The *siddhis* resulting from austerities are far better. The fifth source of *siddhis* is Kundalini awakening by Guru's grace. When the Kundalini rises upward to meet Shiva, in the *sahasrara*, it brings a very great *siddhi*.

JL: You refer to temporary *siddhis*. Which plants do they come from?

Baba: They are derived from several rare herbs, known only to yogis.

JL: At present I'm experimenting with isolation tanks. When one remains inside these tanks for a while, body-consciousness disappears. This sort of isolation tank has also been tried by astronauts.

Baba: I meditated in a room for a long time, and as a result that room is more powerful than your tanks. It is my special tank. Someone sitting in it can still hear the mantra I practiced.

In India, people dig pits forty feet deep and sit inside to obtain great *siddhis.* The trapdoor is covered from above with earth. Is your tank like that?

JL: Ours is more simple. In America, we want instant experience; so we are building samadhi tanks.

Baba: How big is your tank?

JL: Three meters in length, two meters wide, and one meter deep. One can sit in it or lie down—whatever one wants.

Baba: Yogis, when they bury themselves under the earth, suck in air by means of special pranayama techniques.

JL: Do they eat?

Baba: The air is their food.

JL: What about excretion?

Baba: Air doesn't produce any excrement, and one can draw strong food from the air.

JL: What about water?

Baba: No matter how dry the air is, it still contains some moisture. In the modern age, science has developed many *siddhis;* iron flies in the air and floats in the water, but the bliss of the Self is the greatest *siddhi.* I notice that you have studied Patanjali's *Yoga Sutras* very carefully. You must have read about *samyama,* the three-fold process of concentration, meditation, and absorption, through which *siddhis* are obtained. There is another book, *Pratyabhijnahridayam,* which is a short work but divinely inspired. You should also study that.

There are many scriptures, but more important than scriptural knowledge is direct experience. In the Upanishads, there is a good analogy about a ladle used for serving sweet pudding. This ladle goes around offering the pudding to everyone, but if you asked the ladle what the pudding tastes like, it wouldn't know because it only serves the pudding—it has no tongue.

JL: We ask the ladles to come to us and sit in our tanks and find out what is inside of them.

Baba: It is true, one must see the inner world.

Dr. Harold Puthoff and Dr. Russell Targ, physicists doing research in psychic phenomena and psychic energy at Stanford University Research Institute, came to the Oakland Ashram to speak with Muktananda. They are also doing work with laser beams. This was explained to the Swami as the two men were introduced.

Baba: Our ancient Hindu epic, the Mahabharata, describes events similar to the firing of missiles into space. In those days there were beings whose power extended as far as the moon and sun, but such people don't exist any more. Their missiles were very small, and they could hit even a distant target with great accuracy. They created weapons by the power of mind and the power of mantra. In those days saints and seers lived such austere lives that they acquired those powers, which come from extreme inner purity. Nowadays, people seem to think that machines can give them whatever they want; so they don't attach much importance to purity. Perhaps they don't think they need it. Yet even now a few people have acquired great spiritual power, and they can perform fire rituals in which the fire is kindled by the use of mantras instead of matches. In the yogic tradition there have been many extremely powerful people—my Guru, for example. He only had to throw something at you and you would immediately fall into a meditative state. Such people gain their power by remaining pure and truthful and without desire. For the most part, they have been renunciants. Even my Guru's samadhi shrine contains powers of this sort.

Dr: There are many people who come to work with us in addition to physicists, and we find that a few of them have some sort of power over material objects. Can you explain this?

Baba: Such petty miracles are very ordinary. Highly advanced beings can do things like that and more. When my Baba visited an electrical power station, he caught hold of a live wire with both hands just to show what would happen. The flow of electric current completely stopped, and he didn't even get a shock. Our body contains small amounts of a similar electricity, and when we practice deep meditation, we feel its presence. But there is an even greater power than this ordinary electric force in our body.

Dr: We know from our research that the currently accepted picture of space and time—reality in general—is not accurate. Can you tell us what kind of experiments we could undertake in order to obtain a true picture of reality?

Baba: If you wanted to get a true picture of space and time, you would have to spend as much energy going within yourself as you do experimenting with all these material objects. There is a center of pure knowledge in the heart called *shuddha vidya.* When you reach the heart center through meditation, that center opens and you get a true experience of time and space. Many saints have had this experience.

Dr: We see our work as a breakthrough in bringing to our materialistic culture the awareness that spiritual elements are involved in even physical life. Do you have any guidance as to which areas should be avoided, from an ethical viewpoint, and which should be investigated?

Baba: Supreme Consciousness is supremely free; therefore, it can never fall into the hands of any one person or be controlled by instruments. You can experience it in the cerebral center called the *sahasrara* in the form of a blue dot, which resembles a pearl. Although it is visible, it is so subtle that no one can touch or influence it.

HP: I have seen that small blue dot at times.

Baba: That's possible. It appears to people who are pure and simple-hearted. I can see in your face the capacity for that experience. You might have accumulated merit in past lives because of which you have attained a high position in the sciences and become worthy of seeing the Blue Pearl. It may well be that some ancient rishis and seers have been reborn now as scientists.

But one's work is not completed simply because one has had a vision of the Blue Pearl. Man has four bodies, although most of us know only two—the physical body and the subtle, or astral body, which we experience in dreams. The blue dot that you have seen is the fourth, or supracausal body, but just having a glimpse of it is not sufficient. You must analyze it further to understand it fully. Within that tiny dot is hidden the supreme principle, which you can see in meditation as the dot begins to remain steady. The details of this experience were kept secret by our ancient seers so that they could gauge a person's state of inner evolution by testing his own knowledge of these mysteries. It is not possible to determine a person's inner state by simply observing external characteristics, such as the clothes he wears or his knowledge of scriptures, nor is much importance attached to the exhibition of supernatural powers. Only those people who have penetrated and explored the Blue Pearl can be considered to be genuine spiritual beings.

Scientific experiments are fine, but they deal with only a negligible fraction of the power of the Blue Pearl, which causes the whole universe to function. It is the same supreme Consciousness that causes the prana, the vital force of the body, to go in and out. Sometimes, the Blue Pearl assumes the form of a being who appears before the meditator and converses with him. This Blue Person, though very clear and solid looking, is actually composed of blue light. When we respect and adore our Guru, it is not the physical body that we worship but the presence of this luminous Blue Form within our own body. This Blue Person, who resides within the tiny Blue Pearl, is the true Guru. He may communicate a message or talk to us and then contract once more into the original dot. The importance of Siddha Yoga lies in this magnificent little dot. The Siddha Guru can awaken its dormant power by simply transmitting his own fully active power into a seeker. Once this power, this Shakti, is awakened, a person can progress as far as he likes depending only on his capacity and the keenness of his interest.

Dr: In Kundalini meditation, one experiences energy in the body, sees lights, and so on. Is this the same energy that one experiences in the physical universe, or is it a different energy?

Baba: Physical energy is an aspect of this inner energy, which we call Kundalini Shakti. On the one hand, it functions as the vital force which controls our breathing and vitalizes the psychological instruments of mind and intellect; on the other hand, this very same energy appears as the universe itself. In meditation you can actually experience this unity of the inner and outer forms of energy, or Consciousness.

Dr: Is there some way to channel the powerful energy revealed in meditation and do something useful with it?

Baba: Yes, there is, and many have done this. For example, I use this energy to gather hundreds of people together at retreats and meditation courses—we call them Intensives—during which I utilize the energy that I have acquired to awaken the dormant inner energy of others. Psychics and others who appear to possess some sort of supernatural ability use only a fraction of the inner Shakti to do their tricks. Even our most ordinary worldly activities are performed with the help of this Shakti.

Just as water solidifies and assumes the form of ice, so Consciousness assumes a material form—the universe. What is this cloth I am wearing? It is nothing but a warp and woof of threads woven in a particular pattern to assume the form of cloth. In the same way, there exist three aspects, or forces, of vital energy of Consciousness which combine to create the whole universe.

Dr: What are these three qualities?

Baba: Technically they are called the three gunas—*sattva, rajas* and *tamas*—and they are the creative forces of the supreme principle. Let me use an analogy. If you take the number '1' and put another '1' with it, it becomes '11'; if you add another '1', it becomes '111'. It is still composed of the single figure '1'; yet it has multiplied many times. In the same way, one material substance has within it the power to create the multiplicity of all existence. Supreme Consciousness has no attributes; it performs no actions. Its nature is simply to exist. The energy, or Shakti, arising within it acts on its behalf and forges the multiplicity we experience around us in our worldly lives.

When you have seen the person within the Blue Pearl, you acquire an ability to see the underlying unity in every object and being. You feel completely whole, happy, and joyful all the time. I can assure you that nothing is higher than this vision. The light is so pure and soft and gives such contentment that all your other needs vanish. I feel that you scientists will attain something significant through effective meditation on the heart. On the other hand, if you meditate on the *sahasrara,* which is the cerebral center, you may lose your capacity to act in the world, and you may turn completely inward. Therefore, if you want to accomplish things, it is better to meditate on the heart, as it does not obstruct your functioning in the world.

I would be extremely happy if you could integrate your experience of meditation into your scientific work. Pursue that tiny Blue Pearl and explore it. It will work wonders for you. You can even ask questions and the inner Person will answer them in ways that will be extremely useful to you.

Because of this inner reality, we honor and revere our Gurus. After we receive their grace, we don't attach importance to ordinary teachers who specialize in such disciplines as hatha yoga. We don't call them Gurus because the real Guru is the Guru principle which dwells within. This grace-bestowing power has enabled thousands of people to receive my touch and have their inner power awakened. This awakening is the root of spiritual growth. According to the scriptures, one who sees the light of the inner Guru is considered to be pure and sinless.

Q: We appreciate this opportunity to speak with you.

Baba: I have the greatest respect for you because you deal with such abstruse scientific subjects. If people like you did work on spiritual matters, you can imagine what help it would be to the world. Your astronauts have already gone to the moon and brought back useful information as a result of directly observing its surface and appearance. If you could make similar progress in meditation, you would be able to visit not only the moon, but also other planets and celestial planes right within your own heart.

In my talks I emphasize that man should not consider himself to be an insignificant creature. I keep telling people that God dwells right within them. I never get tired of saying these things, for I consider them to be my real worship. God doesn't need temples, mosques, or churches because He already has taken residence right within your heart.

RT: I'm sure that now, after speaking to you, I will begin my meditation practice again.

Baba: It is absolutely essential. Meditation culminates in the experience of the Being within the Blue Pearl, and after that there is nothing left to experience. Do you have the vision of this blue dot often?

HP: It is usually when I am thinking about my work that I suddenly see it.

Baba: Actually, it's coming from inside you—from the center of your skull. In yoga, that particular place is described as a triangle surrounded by the Sanskrit letters *"ham"* and *"sah."*

HP: But the blue dot comes and goes too fast for me to examine it.

Baba: It is extremely subtle and you can't control it. It travels so fast that it can take you from the worldly plane to *Siddhaloka* in the twinkling of an eye. The Blue Pearl can never come under anyone's power. Before you can even think, it will disappear. It appears before you of its own accord, and nothing can make it stay there for long. It moves of its own free will, and if it is pleased with you, it will help you. Through the Blue Pearl, I can know the true character of people who come to see me. Even when I'm giving a talk, I will suddenly glimpse a tiny blue dot hovering over someone's head, and I know that he is a good person.

Dr: There are many stories about people in India who can levitate their bodies. Do such people still exist?

Baba: Yes, there are a few. In South India there is a mountain known as Shri Sailam, and some yogis who live there can do that sort of thing. I used to go there every year for a visit. Now an ashram is being built there by my devotees. There is another such place known as Girnar, and also another one near Tibet.

Dr: Is it possible or useful to tap that energy for ordinary use?

Baba: There is nothing wrong with it. The ancient sages, however, never did. But now interests are changing, and it seems that ultimately the power of physical levitation will be used. Many Indian scientific researchers are also familiar with the scriptures that talk about these matters. I read in an American paper that India is third in the world in scientific research. India is materially poor but wealthy in scientific achievement.

Dr: Do you know why the ancients, even though they had the ability to use these powers, did not? Was it a spiritual reason?

Baba: All I can say is that they were great renunciants and that their aim was to live without desire. They gave so much importance to extreme renunciation and desirelessness that they never used such powers in their daily lives. It is the particular feature of Indian spirituality that we experience the things of the world as temporary, knowing that one day everything will be destroyed. Even now we have rishis and sages in India who live without desire, sitting in one place for long periods of time. Many thousands of people used to come to see my Guru; yet he would sit for hours without moving or paying attention to anyone. The two great beings whose photos you must have seen in our chanting hall, Sai Baba of Shirdi and Zipruanna, were also great renunciants, and they were very powerful. Even today people worship their *samadhi* shrines; they come great distances simply to touch the stones. All these beings went naked or wore rags, and they behaved very strangely. I'm the first one to live like a gentleman. I have begun to tell people that renunciants should wear good clothes; they should look clean and neat because people tend to imitate great beings. If we want people to dress with care and act well, we have to provide an example that they can follow. Our Ashram in India is very large and modern. I built it keeping in mind contemporary customs and the needs of the young people of today. It is a beautiful place, and many young people go there. I tell them to have a clean and pure appearance, to cut their beards, shorten their hair, and wear good clothes.

Dr: That makes you an even greater renunciant because you have renounced renunciation.

Baba: True renunciation is more than simply renouncing outer things. Renunciation should take hold of our hearts. Renunciation should arise from within and not simply be imitated from without.

Dr: We appreciate this opportunity of talking with you.

Baba: I am very happy to have met you. Come here and spend some time in meditation. Come at nine o'clock on any morning which is convenient for you, and you can meditate in my room.

Professor Ramiro Calle is a professor of yoga at the University of Madrid, Spain. He has written many books on yoga and interviewed Baba Muktananda for a book he is writing on Kundalini yoga.

RC: Would you briefly describe Kundalini yoga?

Baba: Kundalini yoga cannot be described briefly because it is such a grand and extensive yoga. Kundalini yoga is inspired and directed by Chiti, the same cosmic energy that sustains and directs the order of the whole universe. This energy moves in a channel at the central core of this complex human body. It has two aspects: inner and outer. The outer aspect sustains the order of one's mundane life. The inner aspect lies dormant, but when it awakens it sustains and directs the process of Maha Yoga, the great yoga. Kundalini yoga is a totally independent autonomous yoga and completes itself fully without the help of any other yoga. It is a self-existent and a self-propelled yoga.

The Kundalini stabilizes and controls all the seventy-two thousand subtle nerves of the human body. When it awakens by the grace of the Guru, it purifies the whole nervous system and makes the body radiant. It dispels all diseases, purifies all the body centers, and makes itself an abode of divine peace within the heart. All the senses are refined, cleansed, and strengthened. As this process culminates, the Kundalini reaches the *sahasrara*, revealing a divine brilliance. Sparkling in the middle of this brilliance in the cerebral center is a dazzling blue dot, which the Kundalini enables one to see. Not only that, but by means of this blue dot, or *bindu,* a yogi is shown the subtle worlds, all the gods and goddesses, and all that cannot ordinarily be perceived by the physical senses. As this process continues, samadhi occurs spontaneously. The *jiva,* the individual soul, is lifted above pleasure and pain. After establishing the aspirant in supreme bliss, the Kundalini becomes tranquil.

This Kundalini is the Parashakti of Parashiva, the transcendent energy of the supreme, auspicious principle. Externally, it inspires the creation of the world; internally, it inspires the yogic process. By means of the independent, self-sustaining Kundalini, Maha Yoga unfolds automatically. This yoga can also be called Siddha Yoga, the yoga of the perfect Masters. It is a synthesis of the four yogas—hatha yoga, raja yoga, mantra yoga, and laya yoga—and it is therefore called Maha Yoga, the great yoga. It can also be called Chiti yoga. Chiti is the primordial Consciousness that is the source and essence of the world.

In answering your question about Kundalini yoga, one could fill an entire book. It is a vast subject.

RC: Can anyone practice Kundalini yoga, or is it necessary to have had previous training in yoga?

Baba: Readiness for Kundalini yoga is essential in the form of *mumukshutva,* an intense, sincere desire for liberation. But even without that, profound love for a Siddha can arouse the Kundalini. Kundalini yoga carries all other yogas in its wake; once it has begun, no other yoga is needed.

RC: Is it possible for a person, even without faith, to awaken his own Kundalini through practice of Kundalini yoga?

Baba: The Kundalini may awaken, but what will the person do if he is without faith? If he is without understanding, he won't progress. He will stop halfway. However, if the Kundalini is awakened by Guru's grace, the grace itself will lead the Kundalini on the proper path; faith will come automatically, in due course.

RC: Are there any dangers in awakening the Kundalini?

Baba: Some people attempt to awaken the Kundalini forcibly through self-effort or by means of hatha yoga. In such cases anything can happen; one can even become mad. But when the Kundalini is awakened by the grace of the Guru, it rises spontaneously and transforms the human body, making it divine. Ultimately, it completes its journey and merges into God.

RC: Can Kundalini be awakened accidentally?

Baba: Yes, but only if an "accident" takes place between a Guru and a disciple. If this accident occurred with a post or a wall or an electric structure, the Kundalini wouldn't awaken. When a disciple who is full of devotion meets a Guru who is saturated with Shakti, the Kundalini is awakened immediately.

RC: What is true initiation? Is it an act through which the Guru initiates the disciple into spiritual life? Does it mean the Guru uses his energy to awaken the disciple's Kundalini? Is it merely a symbolic act?

Baba: Without initiation, all actions and rituals are fruitless. Without initiation, spiritual perfection cannot be attained. Shaktipat is the true initiation. Through it, the Guru transmits his own inner Self, his Shakti, his teaching, and his message directly into the disciple. According to the scriptures, this initiation merges the individual soul into Shiva and annihilates its separateness. Initiation leads to spiritual perfection. How can such an initiation be a mere formality?

A Master whose Kundalini has been completely activated through the grace of the Guru and who has the blessing of the Kundalini can fully awaken the Kundalini of his disciples. To transmit just a partial awakening is not of great import. It's possible for one to experience partial awakening by just being in the company of disciples whose Kundalini has been activated by a Guru. One must also consider how far such an awakening will take a person. There are many in the world who are able to induce a partial awakening, but to awaken the Kundalini effectively, one must have attained complete realization, been blessed by one's own Guru and the supreme Goddess, and received their command to perform Kundalini awakening. One should receive as the gift of his Guru the blessing that empowers him to awaken the Kundalini of others.

A lot of people who met me on my tour of America have told me, "My Kundalini was awakened three years ago, but it has gone back to sleep." That is what happens when one does not enjoy the grace of a perfect Master. Such awakening does not serve much purpose. Only a Guru who has been empowered by the blessing of the goddess Parashakti and his own Guru can awaken the Kundalini permanently. These conditions are indispensable. In America, many of my followers give Intensives and are able to awaken the Kundalini in many seekers. They are able to do this successfully because I have given them my command to do so.

RC: Is it possible for a *jivanmukta*, a liberated soul, to judge the ascent of Kundalini in another person?

Baba: Yes, the stage of ascension can certainly be seen by a liberated being. He can also question the disciple and examine him to ascertain his progress and to find out where and how he is blocked.

RC: Which techniques do you consider most useful to stimulate Kundalini?

Baba: Practices for awakening the Kundalini are not the concern of the disciple. It is the Guru's responsibility to awaken the disciple's Kundalini. The Guru may have certain secret methods, but these are disclosed to one who is ready to attain Guruhood, not to one who is still a disciple.

RC: What do the lights, sounds, and other phenomena that arise in meditation indicate to a seeker? Can these be a product of the imagination of an immature seeker?

Baba: The lights and sounds and other phenomena arise to dissolve a seeker's delusion. They are real. *Nada,* or inner sounds, release the flow of various nectars that impart new strength and agility to the body and cause love to spring up from within. As for the visions of light—the very nature of the Self is light. These lights lead a seeker to his final destination; so how can they not be real? A true meditator sees real lights and hears real sounds, day after day, until he goes beyond them to the final truth. These phenomena seem unreal or or imaginary only to one who has not meditated and who has not had a direct experience of them. Immature seekers may imagine they perceive such things, but when one experiences them directly, there is never any doubt about the validity of these experiences.

RC: Does the illumination of the *sahasrara* entail the automatic attainment of samadhi?

Baba: Yes. The divine light in the *sahasrara* is as brilliant as a thousand suns, but it is not hot. Through sustained contemplation of that divine light, the mind becomes totally still. Then the mind relinquishes thought and the individual consciousness ceases. That state is also called *samadhan* or *samadhi,* total stillness.

RC: How can a yogi obtain the perception of the *Purusha,* the divine Consciousness within him?

Baba: In the process of meditation, the vital fluid rises higher and higher until it becomes stabilized in the *sahasrara* from which, in the course of further meditation, the Blue Pearl emerges. With further contemplation, the blue dot becomes pleased and explodes and reveals the Nila Purusha, the Blue Person. According to Indian tradition, this Blue Person makes one a Guru; He gives one the command to impart knowledge to others. This Blue Being is very great. People hearing of Him wonder how such an immense Being can live within the *sahasrara.* His form is composed of blue light, and the Upanishads describe Him as the "Thousand-Headed Being." One should be able to see the Blue Purusha at least once. He is the inner Guru of all, the supreme principle.

RC: What physical and mental symptoms appear as the Kundalini rises and pierces the chakras, the subtle nerve centers?

Baba: As the Kundalini rises in the body and pierces the chakras, various types of emotions manifest, such as laughter, weeping, love, and desire. Anxieties, latent illnesses, and many different *kriyas,* or yogic processes, also occur. One may even appear to be mad for a short time, but it is not real madness. Heavy sleep, lethargy, and involuntary movements of the body may also occur. Hunger may temporarily disappear and sleep may decrease. The answer to this question, like the first one, could fill a whole book.

RC: Is there a definite correspondence between the chakras and the different nerve plexi in the physical body?

Baba: Certainly. The six chakras control all the nerves of the physical body. The chakras contain their own deities and powers, which inspire the functions of all the nerves.

RC: In meditation, should one concentrate on the chakras?

Baba: There is no need to concentrate on the chakras; one should focus the mind on the desired objective. All the chakras are dependent on the inner Self; they are controlled by the inner light. Concentration on the light of the inner Self will open the chakras automatically.

RC: Can mantra repetition enhance the ascent of Kundalini?

Baba: Mantra is very beneficial because Kundalini loves mantra. The Upanishads describe Her as: *kundalini maha mantra para devatai—* "The supreme Diety, the great mantra." Mantra is Her life-breath.

RC: Is it useful to visualize the Kundalini ascending, as is recommended by some tantric techniques?

Baba: The Kundalini rises of its own accord, so what is the need for visualizing it? Kundalini is not imaginary. It is a real manifestation. It transcends imagination. Inner experiences, inner *kriyas,* and inner yoga actually manifest as direct experience. There is no need to imagine anything.

RC: Certain doctrines suggest that man is surrounded by a subtle aura, the color of which indicates his character and degree of evolution and that by perceiving the aura an advanced Master can judge a person's intentions and morality. What is your opinion?

Baba: A great soul, by virtue of his inner vision, can enter the heart of any man and thereby know his disposition and intentions. The divine light of the Atman is pure and subtle. It assumes different colors of red, white, black, and blue. It is so pure that it cannot reflect any impurities. This light is present not only in human beings but pervades the entire creation. It shines in every flower, every stick of wood, every animal, and every stone, and it can be perceived by one who has the divine vision. The blue *bindu,* which is the light of Consciousness, is extrememly enchanting. Its delicate, shimmering blue light extends throughout creation and can be perceived everywhere and in everything by one whose inner eye has been opened by the grace of Kundalini. Through this divine vision an awakened soul can know a person's heart; he doesn't have to look at auras.

RC: Can the process of Kundalini awakening be understood in scientific terms, and is it valuable to try to understand the process, not as a substitute for the experience, but as a way of furthering it?

Baba: Only the superficial aspects of Kundalini awakening can be described in scientific terms. For true understanding, a scientist should have the experience of Kundalini awakening; then, perhaps, he would be able to describe it in terms he is accustomed to.

Scientific instruments can study only the physical and psychological aspects of Kundalini awakening, such as its effects on the organs, nervous system, heart rate, metabolism, and so on. The inner, subtle aspects cannot be detected by instruments because Kundalini is an extremely subtle force; it is pure light. A Kirlian photographer came to me and wanted to photograph a part of my body. Finally, I agreed to let him photograph my finger, and when he got the impression back, it showed a ring of dazzling light rays. It is that vibrating light which is transmitted into a person when he receives Shaktipat.

Many psychologists and other people who are involved in investigating consciousness have visited me. They often pose the question, "How can we get people involved in the study of consciousness?" Each one wants to get people interested in Kundalini awakening in his own way. A scientist wants to get them interested through the use of scientific terms and scientifical investigations, whereas a yogi wants to get them interested through yoga.

I have been in America for a few months, and several thousand people have experienced Kundalini awakening. Among them are psychologists, medical doctors, and other specialists, but they have each experienced it differently and, therefore, describe it differently. As a yogi, I describe it in yogic terms. This is why you scientists must have the direct experience yourselves, and then you can describe it in your terms. You should hang out with me for a while and have inner experiences; then you will find out how to explain them in scientific terms.

A Kirlian photographer came and asked permission to photograph Baba's hands. Baba agreed and placed his fingers on the equipment. Very bright auras of light, which looked like a collection of minute rays, appeared on the screen.

Baba: Now if anyone asks me what Shakti is like, I can show this picture and say that these are the rays of Shakti. If I concentrate, more light will be visible. If you took photographs of my toes, you would find even more light there. That light is the light of Consciousness. It is everywhere—within you, in trees, even in a wall. You are not able to see it, but I see it. Just as steam rises from a teapot, the light of Consciousness rises from every object. Steam has no color, but that light is blue. If I touch someone with a finger, the same conscious force in the form of that light enters the person. If I exercised more control, that light would be stronger; your instruments wouldn't be able to bear the force of it.

6

GOD DWELLS
WITHIN YOU AS YOU

"To welcome another man with love and affection is the highest religion," Swami Muktananda often says. "To find God in your own heart is to experience the highest religious truth. And to carry that awareness with you, seeing the same divinity in others, is to manifest it in your daily life."

Like all great holy men, Baba Muktananda fosters a sense of unity among people and does not cultivate religious differences. He is not a religious politician. Looking at the world from his perspective of unity with God, he experiences all people as part of God's family and thus as part of his own.

When Baba was in Piedmont, California, Father Joseph Scerbo, a Catholic priest, invited him to speak at the Pacific School of Religion. Introducing him to the group of theology students, Father Scerbo said, "Swami Muktananda's visit is a very great event for the whole theological community. Though from outward appearances—dress and language—he looks like a Hindu, you will perceive something in him that is very close to your own heart. A certain light is emitted through Swami Muktananda, and that light has touched my heart. It has opened the door of my heart, and now the mysteries of my own religion have revealed themselves to me.''

People of all faiths and religious traditions came to meet Baba, and many expressed the concern that the practice of meditation would interfere with their own religious practices. Baba assured them that meditation on the Self would not conflict with any particular religious beliefs. ''You may be a Christian or a Hindu or a Moslem or a Jew now, but what were you when you were born? When you are a baby, one or another religion is forced on you. But when you die, you will leave everything behind and depart from the world in the same condition as when you came. These religious distinctions were created only for the purpose of your worldly activities. The inner Self is the same in all people. No religion can claim it or impose any distinction on it.''

Leaders of various faiths and spiritual traditions come to discuss spiritual matters with Swami Muktananda, and they readily agree that the basic teachings laid down by the founders of great religions have often become obscured in dogma and corrupted by politics.

In Oakland, a Jesuit priest who had visited India came and told Baba that he liked Indian spirituality very much and he wanted to assimilate it into his own life. The priest assured Baba that he had faith in his own Christian traditions but was willing to incorporate constructive concepts from other religions.

Baba appreciated the priest's attitude and told him, ''There is one secret in religion: if one has faith in his own religion, he also develops faith in other religions; but on the other hand, if he lacks faith in his own religion, he will become involved in conflicts with other religions.''

Swami Muktananda has had the ultimate experience of union with supreme Consciousness and because he dwells continuously in that state and reflects it in his words and his actions, he is able to transmit spiritual awareness to others. Once a man complained that he had followed many different spiritual paths and had been meditating, but he had never had an experience of God-consciousness. Baba took him into a meditation room, pressed him between his eyebrows, and told him to sit quietly. Some time later, the man returned to the *darshan* room and told Baba, ''When you touched me between the eyebrows, I felt a fire there.''

Baba told the man and the other visitors present, ''My body is full of that fire. That is the fire of yoga. When I say yoga, I mean true yoga, not a mockery of yoga or a few postures. If you meditate, you will feel this fire being released inside. It is the fire of yoga, the fire of love, the fire of true religion, the fire of God.''

The following conversations are just a few of the many that took place between Swami Muktananda and visitors from a wide variety of spiritual disciplines and traditions.

When Swami Muktananda visited Chicago, a group of religious leaders gathered to meet him. Included in the group were Indian swamis, a Lutheran clergyman, ministers from Presbyterian, Episcopalian, and Congregational churches, and Jewish rabbis.

Minister: Do you have a special message for the people of America?

Baba: My message is the same for all the people of the world: Man should give up seeking peace, happiness, and fulfillment in the outside world, because these things lie within man himself, not in some other place. No matter how many luxuries we acquire or how much pleasure we pursue in our waking state, the result at the end of each day is that we feel exhausted rather than fulfilled. So to remove our fatigue, we must abandon all that we have acquired and go to sleep. Man's need for sleep proves that turning within brings far more peace and fulfillment than the pursuit of external things. By turning within through meditation, man can discover the great Shakti, the flame of God, which dwells within his very heart.

Q: Is there a name for your movement?

Baba: In India, it is called Siddha *marga*, the Path of the Siddhas. On this path spiritual growth takes place automatically after you receive the grace of a fully realized Master. That is why it is called the Siddha Path, the path which has been taken by great beings.

Rabbi: What is your understanding of evil?

Baba: What you call evil is inherent in the structure of the world. The world is composed of three gunas—*sattva*, or purity; *rajas*, or activity; and *tamas*, or dullness and inertia. These are the three basic modes of manifestation, and at different times one or another of these forces is predominant. In the Gita, the Lord says to Arjuna, ''O Arjuna, you should transcend the three gunas and reach that place inside beyond good and evil.'' The purpose of all religions is to help you to conquer these gunas. Both good and evil arise from the same principle. The Consciousness from which bliss and purity originate is the Consciousness from which brutality, evil, and insensitivity originate. Our scriptures say that through prayer and other spiritual techniques one should try to become free from the three gunas. If we happen to fall sick, we take some medicine to get rid of the sickness. Likewise, if we have been born into a condition in which there is a lot of evil, we can get rid of it by using God's medicine.

Minister: In the West, there is an absence of the feeling of God within. The scriptures say that the God within is the hope of glory. I would like to thank you for your influence on the West by teaching that God lives within us. Do you feel that the power of Christ in the outer world can function as the inner guru and open up the Shakti in the heart?

Baba: If you have deep love for Christ in your heart, the dormant Shakti will be easily awakened. There is not much difference between the inner Guru and the outer Guru. When you appear to worship the outer Guru, the truth is that your worship is reaching the inner Guru. Whatever you do for God, or seemingly for God, such as opening up your heart to Him, it is, in fact, you who receives the benefit inside yourself. The *Guru Gita* says that in the *sahasrara*, the thousand-petaled spiritual center in the cerebrum, there is a triangle, and in the middle of that triangle lives the Guru—the inner Guru. That Guru is supremely effulgent; the brilliance of his light equals a thousand suns. The only difference is that the light of the outer sun is heating, whereas the light of the inner Guru is cooling. The inner Guru reveals himself to everyone who meditates and gets into higher states of meditation. That Guru exists in the midst of the divine light, in the form of a blue dot called the Blue Pearl, which vibrates there all the time. When you receive the message of truth from the Guru within, you become aware that the outer Guru you have been worshiping is no different from the inner Guru. Seek that inner Guru, visit that inner Guru, because at some time he will also speak to you. The inner Guru is the same for all people of the world, regardless of their religion or race. If you like, you can consider Christ as the supreme Guru who dwells within everyone.

Minister: In every spiritual life a little materialism must fall. I am wondering if the Shakti would make one a better bricklayer, a better doctor, or a better baker.

Baba: Your question is beautiful. If after the inner awakening the Shakti did not enable you to function better in your outer life, what would be the point of it? The Shakti that I am speaking about is not an ordinary energy. It is the energy of Consciousness, the divine creative energy which creates the entire cosmos. The same Shakti is dormant within us and becomes active through Shaktipat, after which it is perfectly capable of taking care of our outer lives. In fact, it improves our outer lives immeasurably. With the aid of the inner Shakti a doctor can diagnose diseases without the use of many instruments, a mediocre bricklayer can become an expert in laying bricks, and a musician can pursue music with great ease. A warrior can fight with tremendous vigor, and a baker is able to bake the rays of Shakti into his bread, making the bread very delectable. The Shakti affects not only humans but also animals and plants and trees. You should see the giant mangoes that grow on the trees in our Ashram. When I used to visit our cows, they would quite often begin to give milk spontaneously. Shakti is the energy of enthusiasm, Shakti is the energy of greatness, and Shakti is the energy of joy. It stirs the heart of every creature.

Q: Some people argue that the spirituality of the East is not suitable for the West because of differences between the two cultures. Do you agree?

Baba: To me, East and West are simply distinctions of direction; they don't apply to human beings. It is the same water that flows in the Indian Ocean as in the Atlantic Ocean. And the air that blows through India is the same as the air that blows here. The moon that glows in India is the same moon that is seen here. The experience of pleasure in India is the same as the experience of pleasure here. The experience of pain is the same in both places, as is the experience of sleep. The experience of the waking state, of functioning in the outer world, is also the same in both places. I have found that men of the East are similar to men of the West, just as women of the East are not different from the women of the West. They may speak different languages, but the same meaning is conveyed. Some time ago, an Indian man from Madras had an operation, and he naturally required a transfusion of blood. The blood that happened to match his blood was from an American donor. So how much of a difference can there be between the two?

Minister: Even within Christianity people lose their love by defending dogma. All over the world I have heard people declare that their religious tradition is the only way. Why do these many paths build walls rather than understanding between men?

Baba: Paths are merely paths. The temple of the Lord lies beyond all paths; so if you want to enter the Lord's temple, you have to leave the path behind. If you stay on the path, you cannot enter the temple. At the same time, all the different paths should be honored because they lead toward the same God. People who embrace religious hostility or bigotry are not religious; they are antireligious. All religious distinctions are man-made. To me, if a religion teaches hatred for other religions, it is not a religion; it is anti-religion. True religion transcends all such distinctions. No particular religion could have a trademark on God because all religions are God's own.

I welcome you all with all my heart. I am very happy to have had this opportunity to meet with different religious leaders. I welcome all religions.

A minister from a Congregational church in Los Angeles, Dr. Edwin Roberts, came to meet Swami Muktananda and discuss various aspects of spiritual life.

Dr. Roberts: How do you maintain constancy in spiritual life? How do you avoid the highs and lows, the ups and downs? In Christianity we have the idea that the spirit comes and goes; yet, in you we feel the presence of spiritual constancy. We all strive for that, but are not able to attain it.

Baba: You find total constancy in Jesus' own life.

ER: Yes, but he wasn't able to communicate that to his disciples. Peter had great moments, but he also had bad moments.

Baba: Our scriptures describe a state of steady wisdom—the illumined state. Through meditation and yoga, the intellect becomes established in that state, and no matter how often things go wrong in the outside world, you are not affected. Through meditation we attain a certain state, which we call witness-consciousness. Once that witness-consciousness is attained, the mind becomes steady and transcends pleasure and pain, joy and sorrow. The Gita says that a true devotee does not feel persecuted, no matter how much people persecute him, nor does he cause others any suffering.

ER: How do you get there?

Baba: For that you need Guru's grace. Through Guru's grace and meditation, you get into that state.

ER: How does the Guru's grace occur?

Baba: By a disciple's love for the Guru.

ER: Is the Guru established in the innermost nature of God all the time?

Baba: Yes, and it is only after one becomes permanently established there that we call him a Guru.

ER: Is there a way in which you can determine your next existence?

Baba: Our next life is determined by the kind of deeds we do and by what we give our hearts to in this life. The *Gita* says that after death you become whatever your mind is set on at the moment of death.

ER: What will be your next existence?

Baba: It appears as though any more births for me have been canceled.

ER: Does that mean that you are now free from human birth and death?

Baba: Well, when God cancels them, there is no question of further births and deaths. If God cancels you, he doesn't want to get any more work out of you.

ER: Is that the goal, then, to get canceled?

Baba: Yes, yes. You have a nice sense of humor!

In Los Angeles a minister of the Church of Religious Science and his wife came to question Baba on the subject of divine love.

Q: Our religion and yours are the same in that love is the main teaching in both. We are told that we must love God supremely, with all our heart and mind and soul, but this is a big order. To be honest with myself, I cannot say that I do love God supremely yet, but I am told that I must if I am to experience bliss and communion with God. Also, I am supposed to love my enemies and those who hurt me. Where is the power to do all this? If I already had this power, I wouldn't need a Master, and I wouldn't need to seek God.

Baba: That love is there within you. You must seek it out.

Q: You mean it is already there?

Baba: It is in the kingdom of the heart. What did Jesus say? He said that the kingdom of heaven, the kingdom of love, is within you.

Q: I know.

Baba: Jesus said that because he had real experiences of the inner kingdom. If you experience that love in your heart, you will be able to understand what Jesus said.

Q: But how do I get the experience? I know the difference between talking about it and experiencing it.

Baba: You should learn to meditate and pray intensely to the Lord within, again and again.

Q: Will that awaken the love in my heart?

Baba: Love will flow out through you. Once you realize love in its fullness, you are able to give everyone that love. You can give something only if you have it to give. You have to find it within yourself. There is a certain way in which it can be tapped. You should keep praying to the Lord and leave everything to His will. When He wills it, you shall find it.

Q: That love is revealed only if it is God's will?

Baba: Yes, but you don't have to just sit idly until that happens. You should offer what little love you have to God and keep doing your *sadhana*. If you want something from a superior, you go down on your knees and implore him until you get it. Likewise, if you haven't yet received the love of God, you should implore Him intensely.

Q: This is a great mystery. I have love, and yet I can't find it. I also have both understanding and the kingdom of God within me, yet I can't find them either.

Baba: This is the greatest marvel of creation. We have forgotten our own true nature and, driven by that forgetfulness, spend our lives looking for the bliss that is already our truest nature.

Q: Thank you for coming to this country.

Baba: I am wondering how I can thank you for having such beautiful hearts.

Q: You see something that I don't see.

Baba: What can I do? I see in you what I see in myself. How can I see anything else?

Rabbi Zalman Schachter, a Hassidic Jew from Winnipeg, Canada, came to Piedmont with several of his students to discuss religious discipline in modern times. He had studied Indian philosophy and, in the traditional manner, brought Baba an offering—flowers, a loaf of freshly baked bread, and a book of Hassidic sayings.

Baba: There is great affinity between Judaism and Hinduism; they are like brothers. Their commandments are very similar. In both traditions purity is strongly emphasized, and it is because of this that the intelligence of Jews is quite sharp. They have produced great researchers, businessmen, and writers such as Einstein and Freud.

Rabbi: One thing I am concerned with is the responsibility of the spiritual teacher. It seems to me that each generation has its own special needs, and when you take the teachings of one generation and just pass them along to the next, it may be that you are not giving young people what is good for that time.

Baba: It's true; there are certain basic aspects of religious tradition that can be changed and should change, from time to time, such as how to conduct yourself, what style of clothing to wear, and so on.

Rabbi: Sometimes the people of the older generation insist that their code of conduct be imbibed before one can imbibe the concepts of prayer and devotion. They want life to be just as it was in the past.

Baba: We have to be very realistic. What has become outmoded and mere empty ritual should not be imposed on the new generation. We have to see what will be conducive to young people's growth and then apply only those aspects of religion which will help them grow. In India, people are sick of empty religion and orthodoxy, and this seems to be the case here in America too. Nonetheless, strict religious discipline is essential for spiritual growth, but it cannot be imposed on people who can't bear it. In order to be willing to endure hardship in one's spiritual practice, one must be passionately dedicated to spiritual life. For example, during my *sadhana* I lived for some time in a Bombay cremation ground because I didn't have any other place to stay—and I didn't mind it. Now, we have a beautiful Ashram in Ganeshpuri with all the modern facilities, but still some people complain that they find the discipline much too hard and that we are much too fierce with them.

At another time during my *sadhana*, I lived under a toilet, which was supported by four pillars, and I put a kind of screen around them. The father of my translator, Malti, is quite rich now, but in those days he was working as an assistant in a restaurant. In the evening, he would bring me some snacks which were my food for the day, and I was quite content with that. In spite of these hardships, I, and people like me, have attained something and have been able to accomplish something meaningful in the world.

We think we are helping the younger generation by trying to make things easy for them, and the result is that they don't do what we call *tapasya*; they don't learn to bear austerities or hardships. The fact is that if you dilute the discipline, realization is also diluted. In the attempt to make things easy, what seems to be happening is that people are not attaining anything.

Rabbi: I am very grateful that you use the scalpel of discrimination to cut away mere custom from real spiritual work. There is a saying in our scriptures: "You should charge the same price for something that you yourself have paid for it." That is the law; you can't make it cheaper.

Baba: If you make it cheaper, you will sustain a loss. There is so much hardship in pursuing worldly life, but when it comes to religious practices, people want everything to be soft and easy. They demand that the discipline be diluted. But I would like to ask: do they dilute their worldly discipline? In worldly life, people work hard, twelve hours a day from morning to evening, for themselves. Shouldn't they be willing to work hard—just for one or two hours—for God? To get just an ordinary B.A. or M.A. degree, one must work many years and study many books. So, for religious life, shouldn't you be willing to study at least half of the *Bible?* You may not study all eighteen chapters of the *Gita,* but at least study one of them. How can you make it easier? We should really think about it, particularly those people who want to dilute discipline and make things very, very easy. Just to be able to fill one's belly, one works for twelve hours or longer; shouldn't one be willing to work just one hour a day to find peace in the heart?

You can make certain external aspects easier, but as far as the inner truth of religion is concerned, you can't do anything about it. It is what it is. Ironically, you find young people all over the world wanting religious discipline made very, very easy, while their worldly life is becoming more and more complex.

Father Scerbo, a modern Catholic priest, visited Baba Muktananda often and had very powerful spiritual experiences. The following conversation took place during their first meeting in Piedmont.

Father Scerbo: Could you explain a technique for expanding awareness?

Baba: Meditate on the inner Self. Along with that, you should also study spiritual philosophy. All that you really need to know is that the same Consciousness pervades every object. Combine that awareness with meditation. Meditation is essential. Once the inner Shakti awakens, everything else will follow. A light that is the size and color of this tiny blue flower you have brought, exists in the top of the head, and it should be seen. You can see it through meditation. I have written about that in *Chitshakti Vilas*.

FS: What is the difference between Christian prayer and meditation?

Baba: Meditation is the very last stage of prayer. Where prayer ends, meditation begins. When your mind becomes fixed in the art of praying to God, when your mind becomes totally still, that is the state of meditation. Meditation is also described in some Christian scriptures. Jesus said that the kingdom of God is within you. To go within and see that kingdom is meditation. Meditation is an essential part of every religious tradition.

FS: Does it matter if you repeat a mantra or can you just look at something? There are many ways to meditate. Is one better than the others?

Baba: There are many so-called techniques of meditation that are mere mental exercises. There are people who try to get into meditation by gazing at a tree or a spot or by looking in a particular direction. But real meditation happens spontaneously as a result of grace; you don't have to learn it. Meditation should happen automatically. However, a Guru in whose presence you get automatic meditation is rare.

There are two kinds of meditation: one is with *japa* and the other is without *japa*. *Japa* is mantra repetition. Mantra has great power and is very necessary. If you meditated with a mantra, you would become absorbed very quickly. However, in pure meditation there is absolutely no thought or object in the mind, not even the mantra. But you reach that state only through the mantra. As you repeat a mantra more and more, the mantra begins to disappear, and you get into a state in which you are aware of neither yourself nor God.

FS: How do people get a mantra?

Baba: A mantra is usually received from a Guru. He gives the mantra that he himself has practiced and whose power he has fully realized.

FS: I would like to experience the power of Christ, and I want to know how I can do that more deeply.

Baba: Meditate. You will experience the Shakti from within immediately. Repeat *Guru Om*. *Guru Om* refers to God; *Guru Om* refers to Jesus; *Guru Om* refers to the Self of all.

Chief Nelson Big Bow, head of the Native American Church, met Swami Muktananda in Albuquerque, New Mexico, where he and his family received Shaktipat initiation at an Intensive. Chief Big Bow invited Baba to the Kiowa reservation, where special ritualistic dances were performed in his honor. The head of the Indian nation was very moved by their meetings and said that it was surely the Spirit Itself which had brought them together.

He invited Baba to be the guest of honor at a Kiowa Society Celebration in Lawton, Oklahoma. The pow-wow was attended by five hundred American Indian chiefs of different tribes and their followers. Baba came from Oakland with a group of his devotees to attend the resplendent gathering. He was welcomed by the venerable chiefs, who asked him many questions regarding the Siddha tradition. (see pg. 154)

Chief: Are you a Christian?

Baba: I am neither a Christian nor a Hindu. I am a human being. I belong to God and humanity.

Chief: How did you attain the position of Guru?

Baba: In our tradition, spiritual Masters select disciples and make them into Gurus.

Chief: Is it inherited?

Baba: Yes, in a way it is. My Guru made me a Guru. Just as a professor prepares his students to become professors, so a Guru prepares his disciples to become Gurus.

Chief: As a spiritual leader, do you have the power to heal the sick?

Baba: Siddha Gurus can awaken the inner Shakti or divine energy through their touch. When this inner energy is awakened, diseases are cured automatically.

Several of the chiefs expressed concern about maintaining their cultural traditions because their young people are being influenced by modern ways.

Baba: Your culture will never perish. It will remain permanent. A culture with love, devotion, truthfulness, and fear of God as its essential ingredients will never perish.

Chief: We Indians are the original residents of America. We are always happy to have visitors from other nations. Kindly pray for the welfare of our nation and people and wish us all prosperity and happiness.

Baba: There is a prayer in our *Vedas,* our holy scriptures, which goes: *sarve bhavantu sukhinah, sarve santu niramayah, sarve bhadrani pasyantu ma kascid dukha bhag bhavet*—"May all be happy; may all be healthy; may all see only auspicious sights; may no one experience suffering." Through this prayer we wish well not only for human beings, but for all living creatures.

Chief: May God bless you when you go back to your people. We hope that, through your blessings, we will have no more wars and that we may live in peace.

Baba: We are all members of God's family. We should all live together in love and friendship.

Later, Baba participated in the ceremonial dances, in which he carried an ancient war lance. He was very pleased with the sincerity and simplicity of the American Indian people. At Nelson Big Bow's request, Baba sanctified the grounds by performing a puja, a ritual of worship, with coconuts and camphor. After the ceremonies, Baba was asked to speak to the group of over ten thousand Indians that had gathered for the historic event.

"I welcome you all with great love and respect. To love and respect other men is a great worship. After seeing your ceremonies and the way in which you worship God, I feel that you are closely related to the people of my India.

"A man can belong to any nation, caste, sect, or religion, but he should remember that everyone is a child of God and experience that oneness. Our *Vedas* say that all humanity has taken birth from one single source, called God. He has entered into all of us and is functioning through us. Therefore, we should have great love and respect for all humanity. God originally created different religions to increase mutual love and brotherhood, but these days, we find that religions are creating disharmony and antagonism among people. Religions may be many, but God cannot be many—He is one.

"I am very happy to observe that you have so much respect for religion and that you have preserved your religious foundations. On this occasion, I give my blessings to you all that, through following your own tradition, you will enjoy the bliss of God, the joy of the Self. If man turns within himself and looks at the inner truth even a little, he will come to know that the supreme Lord is right within his own heart, and he will feel extremely happy about this truth."

Cathy Speeth and Claudio Naranjo, spiritual teachers with a sizable following in the San Francisco Bay area, spent a great deal of time with Muktananda in Piedmont. One day, they brought a friend of theirs, Carlos Castaneda, author of the best-selling series of books in which Castaneda chronicles his apprenticeship under a Yaqui Indian sorcerer. Quite naturally, the conversation between Baba and Castaneda focused on a comparison of the traditions of yoga and American Indian sorcery.

Carlos Castaneda: I am very delighted to be here with you, in such holy company.

Baba: In India, it is impressed upon our minds again and again that we must seek the company of yogis, saints, and other spiritually evolved people.

CC: I come from a different tradition. The way that I met Don Juan was not premeditated at all. I am a Catholic, and our only interest in the realm of religion is to conform with dogma; as long as you do that, you are safe. To meet Don Juan was really fortuitous. I was not seeking it. Now, of course, my attitudes have changed. He has shown me that the only way to grow is to seek the company of beings who are on the path of knowledge.

Baba: What you are saying makes a lot of sense. We cannot get inner contentment just by following dogma. If dogma could help us find the contentment that lies beyond it, it might have some use. Jesus said that the kingdom of God is within you. Dogma will justify itself only if it helps you to find that kingdom.

CC: In the case of Don Juan, for instance, there is very little dogma to follow.

Baba: The inner Self is supremely free. It is independent of all external factors, it transcends all rituals, and it is beyond all dogma. In our scriptures, the various philosophical doctrines are called "paths." Now, just as you had to leave the path outside in order to enter this temple, likewise, if you want to enter the temple of God within your own being, you have to leave all the dogmas and rituals outside.

CC: Yes, it requires a complete transformation. I am wondering if you have apprentices or students? I make this distinction: a student is an intellectual, whereas an apprentice is more involved with the practical side of learning.

Baba: You will find quite a few apprentices here. In due course, disciples become like the Guru.

CC: How are they chosen? Is it a matter of the teacher's selection, or are they pointed out by some other, independent force?

Baba: The selection takes place in a most natural manner. As seekers come and visit me time after time, they give expression to more and more of their love, and in this way they choose themselves. It is not a hard task; it doesn't involve much on my part. Once the inner Shakti, the divine energy, touches a seeker and causes an inner awakening, that person is then qualified. I don't have to make a selection; it is the inner Shakti which makes the selection.

CC: That is similar to Don Juan's method. He relies on the spiritual forces to point out an apprentice. The only difference is that once the apprentice is pointed out, the teacher has to trick him into coming for instruction.

Baba: I don't have to trick my disciples into accepting me. The Shakti, which I have received from my Guru, does the work for me, without my willing it. The Shakti passes into a seeker of Her own accord. I don't have to do anything. If you read my book, *Play of Consciousness*, the way in which Shakti grabs people will become clear. This Shakti is also called Kundalini, which is the creative power of the universe.

CC: This process is very different from the way in which sorcerers of the American Indian tradition work.

Baba: There can't be that much difference between the two traditions, because that same Shakti pervades everywhere.

CC: The American Indians believe that no one is willing to undertake a very rigorous training. Don Juan's people feel that a volunteer should be doubted. They believe that the only people who can handle the knowledge are naturally reluctant people, and anyone who volunteers is looked at skeptically. That is why the teacher has to go out and lasso an apprentice.

Baba: We believe that the Shakti, before becoming active in a person, selects him very carefully. This Shakti is the same energy that creates the entire cosmos, and therefore it is very intelligent, very conscious, and all-knowing. She knows past, present, and future, and She knows which people to enter.

CC: Don Juan has had only two apprentices—I am one—in his lifetime, and they came to him when he was at a very advanced age, around eighty.

Baba: Each yogi, or holy man, has a different way.

CC: Do you think there is any difference between the holy quest and what we call sorcery? Is there anything like sorcery or magic in your tradition?

Baba: There is no sorcery or magic in our tradition. In Siddha Yoga, the inner Shakti unfolds itself through meditation, and it is this awakening which grants what are called *siddhis*, or psychic powers. In ancient times, there were yogis who had marvelous and miraculous powers. There was one whose name was Jnaneshwar Maharaj. One day, he wanted to go to meet someone; so he commanded the wall on which he was sitting to move, and the wall carried him to his destination. This is the magic of the inner Shakti, the magic of God's grace.

CC: Yes, I will agree with that. But do you emphasize the practices that lead to the attainment of these powers or are they only incidental to greater development?

Baba: As you go deeper into yourself through meditation, you discover the centers of these powers, and when you come upon them, the various powers make themselves available to you.

CC: Are these centers in the body?

Baba: Not in the physical body; I am talking about subtle centers. There is, for instance, a center in the heart, but it is not the physical heart.

CC: If the centers are not in the physical body, are they in another body?

Baba: Within this body are three more bodies; the subtle centers are situated in those bodies. Right now, you are functioning in one body. When you dream, you enter another body. During deep sleep, you move into yet another body, and when you meditate, you move into still another body. So there are four bodies, not one. According to our philosophy, there are also four corresponding states: waking, dream, deep sleep, and *turiya,* the transcendental state.

CC: I am very curious about these concepts because sorcerers such as Don Juan, in the final ordeal of any apprentice's career, pick up the apprentice and throw him into an abyss. But the apprentice never reaches the bottom. It is difficult for me to understand rationally. What happens to the body? It should smash itself at the bottom of the abyss. Yet Don Juan says that it doesn't. He says that what would make me disintegrate is simply the notion I have about my body being solid.

Baba: According to the yoga of meditation, you pass from gross matter to pure Consciousness. What appears to be gross has emanated from Consciousness. Though the body does not disappear, it loses its grossness and is transformed into Consciousness. We think that it is physical, that it is gross, but in reality, it is pure Consciousness.

CC: Are there steps, in your tradition, that lead to the awareness that everything is Consciousness? Is meditation one of them?

Baba: Our path consists only of meditation. This awareness comes through meditation. As you go deeper and deeper into yourself, you become more and more aware of the fact that you are not gross matter but that you are Consciousness. We call it the different stages of evolution. It appears to me that whatever you do must have roots in our tradition; probably the outer form has changed.

CC: I want to ask you about seeing your own double, which you mention in your book, *Play of Consciousness.* In Don Juan's knowledge, one of the key facets is development of an "outer self"—an exact replica of what we are—which will act in the world for us. Is there anything similar in your tradition?

Baba: Yes, we call it *pratika darshan,* or vision of one's own double. What you describe forms a part of the classic yogic tradition. There have been yogis in India who could exist in two places at once. There was one yogi called Manpuri, who would be in his ashram in one form, and at the same time, would be working elsewhere, in another form. Again, it seems to me that what you are talking about has its basis in our scriptures. The original university, from which these two traditions have come, must be one and the same. If you read our mythological scriptures, you will find yogis or divine incarnations assuming different forms for different tasks which needed to be performed in different places.

CC: Even now, today, is there any emphasis on that practice?

Baba: Yes. Take, for instance, the case of my Guru. Even though he is no longer in a physical body, he often appears to me and gives me advice on different matters. Though he has departed from the physical body, we consider him to be quite real, and we worship him. He appears to us in meditation and dreams, gives us messages, and then goes away. My Guru has revealed himself to many of my followers and given them messages.

CC: Is a real Master one who has transcended his death?

Baba: No one would be regarded as a great Guru in India if he had not transcended death.

CC: How interesting. That is very different from Don Juan's viewpoint. He does not have the concept of transcending death at all. The sorcerers believe that once the body disintegrates, that is the end of everything.

Baba: That is not so. For instance, profound sleep is a kind of death; yet we return from it. At the time of death, we leave only this body, but we do not cease to exist. Whoever has departed from this body can come back in a different body. Would you like to give me an idea of what you do to attain the state which you are supposed to attain?

CC: I have finished my apprenticeship, which lasted fifteen years. Don Juan has now left me; he has thrown me out into the world. Now everything is up to me.

Baba: In India, also, one has to serve as an apprentice for at least twelve years. But there comes a time when the Guru knows that his disciple has become perfect and lets him go.

CC: What you mentioned earlier, about seeing the Master in dreams, is very appealing to me. There was a time when I could meet Don Juan in dreams; but now that he has let me go, I cannot find him anywhere, not even in dreams.

Baba: Some dream experiences bear enormous fruit. What your mind is intensely interested in shows itself in dreams. In India there was a saint called Tukaram Maharaj, and he received spiritual initiation in a dream. As a result of that, he achieved perfection. My own Guru appears to me even now, because to me he is quite alive. I honor him as a living being in my meditation. I love my Guru with all my inner heart; therefore, he appears to me.

CC: Are the dreams in meditation or sleep?

Baba: There are different kinds of dreams. Some are ordinary sleep dreams, whereas others are quite close to meditation, and those are the most dependable dreams. There is also a state in meditation called *tandra,* which is neither dream nor waking, and whatever you see or dream in that state turns out to be true.

CC: So you could have validation of that?

Baba: You are a very good listener. What you say has a great deal of reflection behind it.

CC: For fifteen years Don Juan trained me to listen attentively; so I am always hooked to what is being said—all of me is.

Baba: I can see that.

CC: The only thing I am not doing now is taking notes. I took notes as I talked to Don Juan because he doesn't like tape recorders.

Baba: People like tape recorders because their brains can't absorb what is being said. My Guru didn't like tape recorders either.

CC: Don Juan says that if you have a tape recorder, you are never listening, because you rely on listening to the tape later.

Baba: I agree; but everyone doesn't have the capacity to listen well. It is only rare people who, through long practice, acquire the ability to listen with full attention. Whenever I talked to my Guru I didn't even take notes. Then, when I composed *Play of Consciousness,* whatever I had heard from him rushed up from within and was written down. It was finished in twenty days. Every word he spoke is still in my head.

CC: Yes, I know the feeling. I have the same experience when I try to write about Don Juan, even though I have notes.

Baba: Is Don Juan still alive?

CC: Oh, yes.

Baba: From the account that you have given of him, he seems to be worth meeting.

CC: Yes, and it would be very interesting if he would come to the United States, but he never does. He likes to travel a great deal, but he doesn't go out of Mexico. I have asked him several times to meet various people, but I have never gotten the opportunity to take anyone down to meet him.

Baba: I am very fond of meeting such beings.

CC: We should make an arrangement, but I don't know when I will see Don Juan again. It may be a matter of a few months or perhaps years; he doesn't see me any more. It depends on me now, and on how well I live my life.

Baba: I am very happy that you came here with such love.

CC: I will be back later.

Baba: You will be most welcome; we can meet at any time.

Frederick Rost, an independent writer, came to Pasadena, California, to interview Baba for a book he was writing. His questions were penetrating and inspired Baba to answer very thoroughly.

Frederick Rost: I have read that you are a God-realized man. I would like to know a little bit about what that means in terms that the general public can understand, since "God" means different things to different people.

Baba: God-realization means attainment of supreme bliss. It means overcoming bondage and attaining a divine state. It is the continuing, unbroken awareness that, "I am the eternal consciousness."

FR: You say that you want people to experience God directly. Do you mean God in the absolute, transcendent form?

Baba: You may use any label: God, Brahman, Absolute, Shakti, or Consciousness. It is the same experience.

FR: Does the highest experience of God encompass both the phenomenal and nonphenomenal worlds?

Baba: In the highest experience, one does not perceive any difference between the phenomenal world and the nonphenomenal world. They become identical.

FR: In that state, do you lose the discrimination to see things separately in space, as, for example, the difference between trees and people?

Baba: One perceives differences among such things, but one is also aware that the differences are only apparent. For example, gold ornaments may come in an endless variety of shapes, sizes, and designs, but the jeweler sees the same gold in each of them. In the state of divine Consciousness, one is aware that all things are made of the same conscious energy. In this state, one realizes that it is the same God, the same Truth, which has become all these different objects. What appears to be matter is matter just for a short while; it is really Consciousness, and it merges back into Consciousness. Consciousness and matter are just like ice and water. Water becomes ice for a while, and then the ice melts and becomes water again.

FR: So at some point all objects disappear back into the formless.

Baba: The world remains as it is; it doesn't disappear. But the way in which you perceive it does change. Instead of seeing different objects composed of matter, you see only Consciousness.

FR: But if we see many things at once, we presume that they have all come out of the one source. Is the Absolute one and many at the same time?

Baba: The one becomes many, and the many again merge back into the one. We can take the analogy of an ocean. The water of the ocean takes the form of countless waves, which rise up and then break, the waves merging back into the water. As the cycle begins again, the waves once more begin to form. But the truth is that the ocean and the waves are the same. There is no difference between the two.

FR: So it is the Absolute which becomes both the form and the formless.

Baba: Yes, the Absolute assumes both form and formlessness.

FR: God is therefore both one and many at the same time.

Baba: Yes, depending on your vantage point. You can see Him as the one, or you can experience Him as the many. If you look at the sun from the point of view that it is one, you will see it as one. But if you look at the sun's individual rays, you will see that they are endless. The same is true in relation to God and His creations.

FR: Do you mean that when you are watching the creation you are free from it?

Baba: Not only are you free from creation, but after you have attained witness-consciousness your attitude toward creation changes. Creation is no longer separate from you. You begin to feel, "I am everything, I am God, I am creation."

FR: Then you are the witness and also the creation that you are watching.

Baba: Yes, the seer is also the seen.

FR: Would you say that you are the witness of the creation?

Baba: A being who is established in witness-consciousness does not attach much importance to such a statement. He simply lives there. He is That.

FR: Does he know that he is in that state?

Baba: The inner Self is just like the sun. It illuminates not only other objects, but also itself.

FR: Some teachings say that you can neither talk about nor experience the Absolute.

Baba: This is just a figure of speech. Though the Absolute is far away from the senses, it is also, in a limited aspect, that which makes the senses function and which perceives through the senses. The Absolute has become everything, including the senses and all sense objects. There is nothing else in creation that can take form, and there is nothing else in creation that can remain without form. Through the senses, the Absolute perceives itself in various forms. The basic experience is that you perceive the one in the many and the many in the one. Water is water, and regardless of whether it is perceived as a lake, a river, a well, or an ocean, it is still the same water.

FR: Have you experienced the Absolute state, which is beyond form and formlessness?

Baba: That is the state of samadhi. Everybody experiences this state during certain moments, but a yogi can experience it continually. It is called the state of *sakshibhava,* or witness-consciousness. When one becomes established in the witness state, one constantly perceives everything from an objective distance.

FR: Does perceiving things in this way make you free and eliminate all fear in your life? Is there any fear in your life?

Baba: I have never known fear in my life. Once ignorance is eliminated, the very center of fear is burned up.

FR: Which center is that?

Baba: It is called *avidya,* or ignorance—imperfect understanding of one's nature.

FR: Today in the world many people don't value this kind of understanding. What would you say has caused this decline of interest in spiritual knowledge?

Baba: It is due partly to a lack of the right kind of education and partly to the fact that people are simply not informed about such matters in their daily lives. If a good movie comes into town and is very well advertised, a lot of people will rush to see it, but if no one is told about the movie, no one will see it. Likewise, people are not told about God, so they don't become interested in spiritual knowledge.

FR: Do yogic teachings, which we hear so much about, suggest that we just leave everything to God? Mustn't we do something for ourselves?

Baba: I have surrendered myself totally, and the people who are following me have surrendered themselves, and still we work constantly. Surrender does not mean that you make God work for you. Who says that surrender means to turn God into a cook to cook your food, or into a washerman to wash your clothes, or into a hairdresser to dress your hair, or into a sweeper to sweep your floors? Surrender means offering to God the fruits of your actions, not effort and duty. Surrender means to perform your duties faithfully and not be affected by the results, whether they are good or bad, pleasant or painful. Surrender to God means that you do God's work and follow His law in everything.

FR: Could you tell me about one of your experiences of the Divine, before we close?

Baba: Great divinity lives within man. When by my Guru's grace, I reached the heart center in meditation, I could see the entire cosmos. I traveled from one world to another—worlds such as heaven and hell, and the world of the ancestors. The heart center is most wondrous. In that center I saw and experienced love. I also experienced the center of knowledge, which is the center of all arts. Sometimes I could overhear distant conversations. Sometimes I could also see immediately whether a visitor was a cheat or a genuine person. Now I have transcended all that. From the heart center I moved up to the center between the eyes, and that center would release the most celestial fragrances. When I reached the cerebral center— the highest center—I saw the supreme light blazing, whose brilliance cannot be surpassed by a thousand suns. Then I heard the most melodious harmonies in the spaces surrounding the inner sun, and nothing in the outer world can surpass that music. As I heard those harmonies within, I would get into the state of natural samadhi. In the midst of this light I saw a glorious spectacle—a tiny blue dot—the Blue Pearl. The Blue Pearl is a most magical thing. I would watch its magic with great fascination. Sometimes the dot would explode into the form of Rama or Krishna or some other great being, and sometimes it would appear as just a spot of light. Since I saw that, I see the same thing in everyone. I have become fully convinced that, whether or not he is aware of it, man is great, he is sublime, he is divine. God's glory lives in him in all its fullness. And that is why I welcome you all with all my heart.

FR: I thank you for your time.

Baba: I haven't given this much time to anybody else. You must have done something magical before coming here.

GLOSSARY

ajna chakra: spiritual center located between the eyebrows.

Arati: the waving of lights as an act of worship; a devotional chant sung by devotees accompanied by the waving of lights.

Arjuna: one of the heroes of the Mahabharata epic.

asana: postures practiced to strengthen the body and nerves; a seat or mat for meditation.

ashram: a spiritual institution or community where spiritual discipline is practiced; the abode of a saint or holy man.

atman; Atman: the individual self; the universal Self.

Ayurvedic medicine: ancient Indian science which teaches that good health depends on maintaining the even balance of the three bodily humours: bile, wind, and phlegm.

Baba: a term of affection for a saint or holy man, meaning "father."

Benares (or Kashi, Varanasi): a holy city located on the banks of the Ganges River.

Bhagavad Gita (or Gita): one of the essential scriptures of Hinduism, a portion of the Mahabharata, in which Lord Krishna instructs Arjuna on the nature of God, universe, and Self.

Bhartrihari: poet-saint and King of Ujjain who renounced his kingdom to devote his life to spiritual pursuit.

bija mantra (seed mantra): a basic sound from the Sanskrit language, the repetition of which manifests the object, deity, or state which it represents.

Blue Pearl (nila bindu): the subtle abode of the inner Self.

Blue Person (Nila Purusha): the personal form of God visualized as a Blue Being.

Brahma: the absolute reality manifested as the active creator of the universe.

Brahman: the absolute reality or all-prevasive supreme principle of the universe.

brahmin: the first caste of Hindu society the members of which are by tradition priests and scholars.

chakra (lit. wheel): any one of seven centers of consciousness located in the sushumna nerve through which the Kundalini rises.

Chiti: divine conscious energy; creative aspect of God, portrayed as the universal Mother.

Chitshakti: the power of universal Consciousness.

Chitshakti Vilas (or Play of Consciousness): Baba's spiritual autobiography in which he relates the experiences he underwent on the path of Self-realization.

darshan: seeing or being in the presence of a revered person, sacred image, or sacred place.

dharma: essential duty; religion; the law of righteousness.

Dhruva: boy who performed severe penance to gain a high and eternal position.

diksha: any religious initiation; initiation given by a Guru usually by imparting a mantra; in Siddha Yoga it means the spiritual awakening of the disciple by Shaktipat.

fakir: wandering renunciant.

five elements: ether, air, fire, water, earth.

four bodies: contained in one another: (1) the physical body, experienced in the waking state; (2) the subtle body, experienced in the dream state; (3) the causal body, experienced in the deep sleep state; (4) the supracausal body, experienced in the state of meditation. The four lights associated with each body, which can be seen in meditation, are: red—physical body; white—subtle body; black—causal body; and blue—supracausal body.

four states: the four states of consciousness: waking (jagrat); dream (swapna); deep sleep (sushupti); and transcendental (turiya).

Ganeshpuri: an ancient sacred spot where Swami Nityananda settled, and where Gurudev Siddha Peeth of Swami Muktananda is situated in Maharashtra state, India.

Ganges: the most sacred river in India which flows from the Himalayas.

Garbha Upanishad: one of the Upanishads which gives an elaborate description of the physical body and how the soul abides in it and longs for liberation. see also: Upanishads.

Garuda: the king of birds, the celestial vehicle of Lord Vishnu.

Girnar: a sacred mountain on the west coast of India where many sacred shrines of the Hindu, Buddhist, and Jain religion are found. It is considered to be the divine abode of many great Siddhas.

Gita: see Bhagavad Gita

Guru: In the Siddha tradition, the Guru is the grace-bestowing power of God who initiates disciples through Shaktipat diksha.

Gurudev: a term of address for the Guru, signifying the Guru as an embodiment of God.

Guru Gita (lit. song of the Guru): a garland of mantras in the form of a dialogue between Shiva and His consort, Parvati, which explains the knowledge of the Guru and the inner Self.

Guru's grace (gurukripa): the divine energy bestowed on a seeker through the compassion of the Guru

Hanuman: a monkey of great strength who is revered as the ideal devotee and servant of Lord Rama.

Harigiri Baba: a Siddha saint from Maharashtra who bestowed great love and affection on Baba.

hatha yoga: a yogic discipline consisting of various bodily and mental exercises practiced for the purpose of purifying the nerves.

Indra: the lord of heaven in the Indian mythology.

Indraloka: the subtle realm of heaven presided over by Indra.

Intensive: a two day concentrated program of instruction in the philosophy and practice of Siddha Yoga.

Jagadguru: world teacher.

Janaka: Saint king who was the father of Sita, Lord Rama's consort. His Guru was Yajnavalkya.

japa: repetition of a divine name or mantra.

jiva: individual soul.

Jnaneshwar Maharaj (1275-1296): a great Siddha and child yogi of extraordinary powers. His rhapsodic verse commentary on the Gita, the *Jnaneshwari*, is acknowledged as one of the world's most important spiritual works. He took live samadhi at the age of twenty one in Alandi, Maharashtra, where his samadhi shrine continues to attract thousands of seekers to this day.

Kabir (1440-1518): Siddha and poet who was a householder and lived his life as a weaver in Benares. His followers were both Hindus and Moslems, and his influence was a strong force in overcoming religious factionalism.

karma: physical, verbal, or mental action; one's destiny as shaped by one's previous actions.

Krishna: an incarnation of God, whose life story is described in the Hindu devotional scripture, Shrimad Bhagavatam, and whose spiritual teachings are recorded in the Bhagavad Gita.

kriya: spontaneous bodily movements initiated by the awakened Kundalini. Kriyas purify the body and nervous system so as to allow a seeker to endure the energy of higher states of consciousness.

kumkum: red-colored powder used for putting an auspicious mark between the eyebrows and for ritual worship.

Kundalini (lit. coiled one): the primordial Shakti or cosmic energy that lies coiled at the base of the spine of every individual.

loka (lit. world): a physical or subtle realm of existence.

lotus posture (padmasana): the most important posture for meditation formed by sitting on the ground with the back erect, placing the right foot over the left thigh and the left foot over the right thigh.

Maha Yoga (lit. the great yoga): see Siddha Yoga

Mahabharata: the epic poem compiled by the sage Vyasa which recounts the struggle between the Kaurava and Pandava brothers over a disputed kingdom. As its vast narrative unfolds, a treasure house of Indian secular and religious lore is revealed. The Bhagavad Gita, which contains the spiritual teachings of Lord Krishna, occurs in the latter portion of the Mahabharata.

maha mantra: any great mantra such as Hare Rama Hare Krishna, Om Namah Shivaya, etc.

mahapralaya: the great destruction of the universe when God reabsorbs all names and forms into His being.

Maharashtra: a state located on the central west coast of India in which the Ashram of Swami Muktananda is located.

mahatma: a title, meaning a great being or a great soul.

mantra: sacred words or sounds invested with the power to transform and protect the one who repeats them; God in the form of sound.

nada: divine music or sound; sounds heard during advanced stages of meditation.

nadi: the 72,000 subtle channels of vital force in the body.

Nanak (or Guru Nanak 1469-1538): a poet-saint and a native of the Punjab. His teachings form the basis of the Sikh religion.

nila bindu: see Blue Pearl

Nila Purusha: see Blue Person

nirvikalpa samadhi: the highest state of samadhi beyond all thought, attribute, and description.

Nityananda (lit. eternal bliss): great Siddha Guru who settled in Ganeshpuri, and who is the Guru of Swami Muktananda.

Om: the primal sound; the sound or vibration from which the entire universe emanates.
Om Namah Shivaya: a mantra, meaning "Salutations to Shiva." Shiva denotes the inner Self.

Pandharpur: a place of pilgrimage and the center of worship for the devotees of Vitthal (a form of Krishna), in Maharashtra state.
Parashakti (lit. supreme Shakti): the Absolute in its form as dynamic creative energy.
Parashiva (lit. supreme Shiva): the primal Lord, the supreme Guru.
Patanjali (second century A.D.): sage and author of the Yoga Sutras, the practical exposition of raja yoga.
Prahlada: a child devotee. His devotion angered his father, a demon king, who tried several times to kill the boy. By the strength of his devotion, Prahlada was saved each time by the Lord.
prana: life-breath; the vital force of the body and the universe which sustains life and is the power of animation.
pranayama: various breathing techniques practiced to make the breath steady and thus achieve mental equanimity.
prasad: a gift from the Guru; any offering made to God or the Guru which is then distributed to devotees.
Pratyabhijnahridayam: a concise treatise consisting of twenty aphorisms which summarizes the nondual philosophy of Kashmir Shaivism.
puja: worship
purusha: the individual soul; the indwelling form of God.

Ram Tirth (1873-1906): a Punjabi saint and devotee of Krishna who visited the U.S.A. from 1902-04.
Rama: an incarnation of God whose life story is told in the Indian epic, the Ramayana; a name for the all-pervasive Lord.
raja yoga (lit. the royal yoga): the path of attaining union with the Absolute by following a practical discipline of eight steps as expounded by Patanjali in his Yoga Sutras.
rishi: a seer of Truth; this term is also applied to the sages to whom the Vedas and other scriptures were revealed.

Sadguru: a true Guru, a divine perfect Master.
sadhana: spiritual discipline.
sadhu: a monk or ascetic.
sahasrara: the topmost spiritual center or thousand-petaled lotus located in the crown of the head. It is the seat of Shiva, the supreme Guru.
sahib: a term of respect, meaning "master or lord."
Sai Baba of Shirdi (1838-1918): one of the most popular saints of twentieth century India. His samadhi shrine at Shirdi, Maharashtra, continues to be a popular place of pilgrimage in India today.
samadhi: complete absorption or identification with the Self, meditative union with the Absolute.
samadhi shrine: the tomb of a saint, which is alive with the spiritual power of the saint who is buried there.
Samartha Ramdas (1608-1681): Maharashtrian saint who helped to unify and renew the Hindu religion in Maharashtra when it was threatened by extinction from Moghul invaders. He was the Guru of King Shivaji, the hero-king of Maharashtra.
Samkhya: one of the six orthodox schools of Indian philosophy which presents a systematic account of the process of evolution and views the world as comprised of two ultimate realities: Spirit (purusha) and Nature (prakriti).
samsara: the cycle of birth and death.

samyana: the term used for the union of the following three spiritual practices: dharana (fixed attention); dhyana (meditation); and samadhi (identification with the object of meditation).

sannyasa: a vow of renunciation in which one becomes freed from all worldly obligations in order to devote one's life to the pursuit of Self-realization.

sannyasi: a monk or ascetic, one who has taken the vow of renunciation.

sat-chit-ananda: the nature of absolute reality: sat is existence, that which exists in all times, in all places, in all things; chit is universal Consciousness, that which illumines all things; and ananda is divine bliss.

satsang: a meeting of devotees to hear scriptures, chant, or sit in the presence of the Guru; the company of saints and devotees.

sattvic: having the qualities of harmony, purity, intelligence.

savikalpa samadhi: the state of absorption in an object of contemplation where knowledge of the object is retained.

Shaivism: the philosophical school which describes the nature of reality as the all-pervasive Shiva.

Shakti (or Chiti, Kundalini, Kundalini Shakti): spiritual power; the divine cosmic energy which projects, maintains, and dissolves the universe.

Shaktipat: transmission of spiritual power (Shakti) from the Guru to the disciple; spiritual awakening by grace.

Shankaracharya (788-820): the great Indian philosopher and saint who expounded the philosophy of absolute nondualism (Advaita Vedanta).

Shiva: a name for the all-pervasive supreme reality; one of the Hindu trinity of gods, representing God as the destroyer.

Shivaji (1627-1680): hero-king of Maharashtra who succeeded in uniting the Marathi people against the invasions of the Moghul armies.

Shrimad Bhagavata: a very popular devotional scripture, sacred to Hindus, containing spiritual teachings in the form of legends and stories of gods, kings, and sages as well as the life and teachings of Lord Krishna.

Siddha: perfect one; one who has attained the state of unity awareness and experiences himself as all-pervasive and who has achieved mastery over his senses and their objects.

Siddhaloka (lit. world of the Siddhas): the subtle realm where Siddhas dwell; the state of pure consciousness in which a Siddha abides.

Siddha pitha (lit. the abode of a Siddha): the place where a Siddha lives or has lived which is permeated with the Shakti of that saint.

Siddha Yoga (or Maha Yoga): the yoga that is received by the grace of a Siddha, a perfectly realized Master.

siddhis: supernatural powers attained through the practice of yoga.

So'ham (lit. I am That): the natural vibration of the Self which is sounded spontaneously with each incoming and outgoing breath.

Sri Sailam: a holy place in south India, known as an abode of Siddhas.

swami: title given to a sannyasi, one who has taken the vow of renunciation.

swargaloka: heaven, the celestial region.

tandra: a state of higher consciousness, beyond sleep, which is experienced in meditation.

tantra: an esoteric spiritual discipline which worships Shakti, the creative power of the Absolute, as the divine Mother.

tapasya (or tapa; lit. to heat up): austere or ascetic practices.

thousand-petaled lotus (sahasrara): the spiritual center in the crown of the head where innumerable nadis (subtle nerve channels) converge giving the appearance of a thousand-petaled lotus. It is the seat of Shiva, the supreme Guru.

Tukaram Maharaj (1608-1650): a great Siddha poet-saint from Maharashtra born at Dehu.

Tulsidas (1532-1623): North Indian poet-saint and author of the Hindi version of the Ramayana.

turiya: the transcendental state, the fourth state of consciousness beyond waking, dream, and deep sleep, in which the true nature of reality is directly perceived; the state of witness-consciousness.

turiyatita: the state of consciousness beyond turiya; the supremely blissful state of complete freedom from all duality and the awareness of the one Self in all.

Uddhava: friend and devotee of Lord Krishna.

Upanishads: the teachings of the ancient sages which form the knowledge or the end portion of the Vedas. The goal of life, according to the Upanishads, is realization of Brahman.

Vedanta (lit. end of the Vedas): one of the six orthodox schools of Indian philosophy arising from discussions in the Upanishads about the nature of the Absolute or the Self.

Vedas: the four ancient, authoritative Hindu scriptures, regarded as divinely revealed. They are: Rig Veda, Yajur Veda, Sama Veda, and Athara Veda. They contain codes of conduct for religious and social life.

Vivekananda (1863-1902): the illustrious disciple of Sri Ramakrishna Paramahamsa.

Yajnavalkya: a sage whose teachings are recorded in the Brhadaranyaka Upanishad, and the Guru of King Janaka.

yoga (lit. union): the state of oneness with the Self, God; the practices leading to that state.

yogi: one who practices yoga; one who has attained the goal of yogic practices.

Yoga Sutras: a practical treatise on the science of yoga written by Patanjali in the second century A.D.

Yoga Vasishtha: a great nondual philosophy in which the seer Vasishtha instructs Lord Rama.

Gurudev Siddha Peeth, Ganeshpuri

DIRECTORY

Swami Muktananda has several hundred meditation centers and ashrams throughout the world and many new ones open each month. The list below was accurate as of Sept. 1, 1978. If you cannot locate a center or ashram listed in your area or you are interested in knowing if one has opened in the intervening time, write to S.Y.D.A. Foundation Headquarters, P.O. Box 11071, Oakland, CA 94611, U.S.A. or to any of the major ashrams or major centers which are identified in bold type below. For information on the ashrams and centers in India, contact: Gurudev Siddha Peeth, P.O. Ganeshpuri (PIN 401 206), Dist. Thana, Maharashtra, India.

UNITED STATES OF AMERICA

Arizona

Tucson
2905 N. Camino del Oesta
Phone: (602) 743-0462

California

Alameda
547 Lincoln Ave.
Phone: (415) 522-0861

Aptos
215 Elva Dr.
Rio Del Mar
Phone: (408) 688-1665

Big Sur
Esalen Institute
Phone: (415) 667-2335

Bolinas
P.O. Box 243
Programs held at:
165 Elm Rd.
Phone: (415) 868-1098

Campbell
430 East Central
Phone: (408) 378-7491
or 268-2130

Cazadero
P.O. Box 221
No Phone

Corona Del Mar
1701 Oahu Place, Costa Mesa
Programs held at:
430 Carnation Ave.
Phone: (714) 979-8727
or 642-9642

Corte Madera
5 Alta Terr.
Phone: (415) 924-3618

Fremont
41764 Chiltern Dr.
Phone: (415)651-3552

Long Beach
6332 Vermont St.
Phone: (213) 598-5366

Los Angeles (Ashram)
605 S. Mariposa
Phone: (213) 386-2328

Los Gatos
16585 Topping Way
Phone: (408) 356-4421

Shree Gurudev (Ashram)
19330 Overlook Rd.
Phone: (408) 354-1109

Mendocino
1085 Greenwood Rd.
Phone: (707) 895-3130

Oakland (Ashram)
1107 Stanford Ave.
Phone: (415) 655-8677

S.Y.D.A. Foundation
P.O. Box 11071
Oakland, Ca. 94611

8573 Thermal St.
Phone: (415) 638-1161

Occidental
18450 Willow Creek Rd.
Phone: (707) 874-3101

Ojai (Ashram)
P.O. Box 994
Programs held at:
15477 Maricopa Hwy.
Hwy. 33, Ojai Valley
Phone: (805) 646-9111
or 646-1289

401 N Ventura St.
Phone: (805) 646-5228

Palo Alto
476 Ferne
Phone: (415) 494-6914

Redwood City
542 Laurel St.
Phone: (415) 364-9971

Sacramento
1616 21st St.
Phone: (916) 442-6425
& 442-6794

San Diego
1214 Sutter St.
Phone: (714) 295-1617

San Francisco
710 Sanchez St.
Phone: (415) 285-8213

San Jose
7075 Royal Ridge Dr.
Phone: (408) 997-3499

San Rafael
101 Bayview St.
Phone: (415) 456-8511

Santa Cruz
149 Hammond Ave.
Phone: (408) 429-1046

Sherman Oaks
4215 Beverly Glen Blvd.
Phone: (213) 986-2977

Woodland Hills
6147 Tony Ave.
Phone: (213) 883-2373

Colorado

Aspen
307 Francis St.
Phone: (303) 925-4560

Boulder
1355 Chambers Dr.
Phone: (303) 494-1186

2895 E. College #19
Phone: (303) 449-4689

Colorado Springs
624 North Weber St.
Phone: (303) 475-0750

Denver
58 Washington St.
Phone: (303) 733-0360

Pikes Peak
P.O. Box 6311
Colorado Springs
Programs held at:
1331 West Pikes Peak Ave.
Phone: (303) 633-3929

Connecticut

Cornwall
R.F.D. 115
Phone: (203) 672-6797

Greenwich
52 Riversville Rd.
Phone: (203) 531-9310

Litchfield
Box 668
E. Litchfield Rd.
Phone: (203) 567-5395

New Haven
460 Humphrey St.
Phone: (203) 787-2007
Programs held at
Dwight Hall
Yale University
Phone: (914) 343-8903

185

Stonington
8 Hancox St.
Phone: (203) 535-3521

Weston-Westport
144 Goodhill Rd.
Weston
Phone: (203) 227-3481

Delaware

Newark
P.O. Box 4703
Phone: (302) 731-7555
Programs held at:
24 West Delaware Ave.

District of Columbia

Washington D.C.
2900 Connecticut Ave. NW
#326
Programs held at:
1834 Swann St. NW
483-4849, (301) 530-1009

Florida

Anna Maria Island
P.O. Box L
Bradenton Beach
Programs held at:
2107 Avenue A
Bradenton Beach
Phone: (813) 778-1464

Boca Raton
341 W Camino Real #304
Phone: (305) 368-9258

Fort Walton
419 Corvet St.
Phone: (904) 242-5751

Gainesville (Ashram)
1004 SW First Ave.
Phone: (904) 375-7629

1925 N.W. 33rd Ave.
Phone: (904) 372-7686

1622 NW 52nd Terr.
Phone: (904) 373-5683

Jacksonville
2130 Dellwood Ave #1
Phone: (904) 641-3597

Miami
8264 SW 184th Terr.
Phone: (305) 253-3336
& 253-3337

Pensacola
1625 Blvd. Mayor #F4
Phone: (904) 932-9721

Sarasota
620 Corwood Dr.
Phone: (813) 351-2147

Tallahassee
1639 Fernando Dr.
Phone: (904) 224-4282

West Palm Beach
5114 El Claro Dr., S.
Phone: (305) 689-9247

Georgia

Atlanta

P.O. Box 13792
Programs held at:
1036-1 Noble Vines Dr.
Clarkston
Phone: (404) 294-4965

P.O. Box 76584
Programs held at:
3503 Piedmont Rd. N.E.

Macon
605 Poplar St.
Phone: (912) 745-6310

Hawaii

Hawaii
P.O. Box 1573
Phone: (808) 955-6264

Honolulu
5660 Haleola St.
Niu Valley
Phone: (808) 373-4881

34 Gartley Pl.
Phone: (808) 595-7073

Lanikai
151 Lanipo Dr.
Phone: (808) 261-0411

Maui
P.O. Box 1813
Phone: (808) 878-1430

Waikiki
Apt. 2144
1777 Ala Moana Blvd.
Phone: (808) 955-6598

Illinois

Aurora
520 North Ave.
Phone: (312) 851-3044

Chicago (Ashram)
2100-W. Bradley Pl.
Phone: (312) 549-7036

2422 N. Drake
Phone: (312) 486-6595

468 W. Deming
Phone: (312) 549-5195

Cobden
RR2
Robin Hill Farm
Phone: (618) 893-2768

Des Plaines
7843 W. Lawrence
Norridge
Programs held at:
750 Cavan La.
Des Plaines
Phone: (312) 453-1186
& 825-0011

Indiana

Bloomington
2521 Eastgate Ln.
Phone: (812) 339-4901

Indianapolis
5427 Seneca Dr.
Phone: (317) 251-9526

South Bend
733 W. Washington St.
Phone: (219) 287-6147

Kansas

Topeka
7523 Adams RT2
Berryton
Phone: (913) 862-2509

Wichita
3434 Oakland
Phone: (316) 685-5886

Kentucky

Louisville
817 Lyndon La.
Phone: (502) 425-1606

Louisiana

Baton Rouge
3299 Ivanhoe
Phone: (504) 343-6156

New Orleans
5608 Arlene St.
Metairie
Phone: (504) 455-3053

Maryland

Baltimore
P.O. Box 3290
Catonsville
P.O. Box 3237
Phone: 744-7643

Programs held at:
7204 Fairbrook Rd.
Baltimore
Phone: (301) 265-8424

Catonsville
1906 Rollingwood Rd.
Phone: (301) 744-0652

Massachusetts

Andover
45 Whittier St.
Phone: (617) 475-0966

Boston (Ashram)
301 Waverley Ave.
Newton
Phone: (617)964-3024

Glouscester
T.O.H. Apartments,
Bldg. 11, Apt. 7
Essex Ave.

Northampton
25 Franklin St.
Phone: (413) 584-8167

Pepperell
32 Tucker St.
East Pepperell
Phone: (617) 433-9230

Stockbridge
South Lee Road
P.O. Box 793
Phone: (413) 298-4915

Wenham
3 Meridian Rd.
Phone: (617) 468-1311

Michigan

Ann Arbor (Ashram)
902 Baldwin
Phone: (313) 994-5625
& 994-3072

3542 Pheasant Run Cir.
Phone: (313) 971-0271

Kalamazoo
1012 Oak St.
Phone: (616) 381-8355

Milan
12925 Whittaker Rd.
Phone: (313) 439-8249

St. Clair
315 Orchard Rd.
Phone: (313) 329-9178

Missouri

Kansas City
5615 Harrison St.
Phone: (816) 363-5276

St. Louis
1722 A Yale
Richmond Hts.
Phone: (314) 781-8706
Programs held at:
4154 Enright
Phone: (314) 652-3374

Montana

Bozeman
804 S. Black
Phone: (406) 587-8825

Nebraska

Scottsbluff
87 Michael
Gering
Phone: (303) 632-2917

New Jersey

Freehold
412 Woody Rd.
Phone: (201) 780-9150

Jersey City
413 Bancroft Hall
509 W. 121st St.
New York NY
Programs held at:
91 Lexington Ave.
Jersey City NJ
Phone: (212) 865-8475

Upper Montclair
489 Highland Ave.
Phone: (201) 783-9261

Warren
6 Casale Dr.
Phone: (201) 647-5769

Whippany
9 Handzel Rd.
Phone: (201) 887-1483

New Mexico

Las Vegas
P.O. Box 3038
Phone: (505) 425-7315

Santa Fe
156 Rendon Rd.
Phone: (505) 983-7652

Rt. 3 Second Village-B
Phone: (505) 982-9529

Rt. 4, Box 50 C
Phone: (505) 988-3639

New York

East Hampton
11 Milina Dr.
Phone: (516) 324-0950

Jamestown
40 Wescott St.
Phone: (716) 485-1428

Mahopac
22 Putnam Professional
Park
Phone: (914) 628-7597

Middletown
118 Monhagen Ave.
(914) 343-2304

Poughkeepsie
2 Barclay St.
Phone: (914) 473-3307

Rochester
291 Pond Road
Honeoye Falls
Phone: (716) 624-3437

Syracuse
865 Ackerman Ave.
Phone: (315) 475-1837
& 422-2890

Yonkers
30 Locust Hill Ave.
Phone: (914) 965-3461

New York City

Brooklyn
169 Greenpoint Ave.
Third Floor
Phone: (212) 389-6058

473 Humbolt St.
Phone: (212) 383-1488

Manhattan (Ashram)
324 W. 86th St.
Phone: (212) 873-8030

233 W. 83rd St.
Phone: (212) 787-4908

429 East 52nd St.
Phone: (212) 753-4276

115 E. 96th St. #19
Phone: (212) 348-8413
or 628-6094

87-89 Leonard St.
Phone: (212) 925-4718
or 349-2851

110 West End Ave. #3E
Phone: (212) 595-2958

Queens
117-14 Union Tpk.
Programs held at:
22 Kew Gardens Rd.
Phone: (212) 268-2248
Programs also held at:
115-25 Metro. Ave. #144
Phone: (212) 268-2248

68-20 Selfridge St. #5F
Phone: (212) 261-9792

Riverdale
4901 Henry Hudson Pkwy
#5E
Phone: (212) 884-7940

Staten Island
32 Fort Hill Circle
Phone: (212) 273-6460

Ohio

Cincinnati
157 Ridgeview Dr
Phone: (513) 821-3629

Columbus
173 E. Tompkins
Phone: (614) 268-6739

Oklahoma

Norman
1501 Parkview Terr
No Phone

Oklahoma City
3 S.W. 33rd St.
Phone: (405) 632-1366

2733 NW 15
Phone: (405) 947-6060

Oregon

Eugene
1950 Buck St.
Phone: (503) 687-0571

Portland
6027 N.E. 22nd.
Phone: (503) 281-4873

Salem
2995 Perkins Rd. N.E.

Pennsylvania

Erie
3525 Windsor Dr.
Programs held at:
3253 Pine Ave.
Phone: (814) 833-8894

Meshoppen
Box 113, Noxen
Phone: (717) 298-2467

Philadelphia (Ashram)
6429 Wayne Ave.
Phone: (215) 849-0888

Rhode Island

Providence
1269 Chalkstone Ave.
Phone: (401) 861-7482

South Carolina

Columbia
312 S. Bull St.
Phone: (803) 771-6499

South Dakota

Rapid City
1916 Hillview Dr.
Programs held at
1525 Forest Court
Phone: (605) 342-6109

Tennessee

Oak Ridge
712 S. Main St.
Clinton
Phone: (615) 457-2203

Memphis
810 Washington Ave.
Apt. 803
Phone: (901) 525-2704

Texas

Austin
702 West 25th, #9

Dallas (Ashram)
208 McKinney
Richardson
Phone: (214) 690-6736

Dripping Springs
Star Rt. 1-B, Box 92
Phone: (512) 858-7045

Houston
1640 Harvard
Phone: (713) 862-8411
& 443-6587

811 Branard St.
Phone: (713) 529-0006
& 667-2241

Vermont

Chester
P.O. Box 22
Phone: (802) 875-3412

Virginia

Louisa
P.O. Box 545
Phone: (703) 967-0274

Norfolk
749 W. Princess Anne Rd.
Phone: (804) 625-9379

Roanoke
3534 Hershberger Rd. NW
Phone: (703) 563-5905

Washington

Bellingham
2908 Lincoln St.
Phone: (206) 676-0543

Bremerton
2509 E. Phinney Bay Dr.
Phone: (206) 377-2046

Mercer Island
2815 67th S.E.
Phone: (206) 232-1575

Richland
2304 Enterprise Dr.
Phone: (509) 946-7573

Seattle
3721 Meridian Ave. N.
Phone: (206) 632-1484

15709 25th S.W.
Phone: (206) 242-1151

6006 2nd Ave. N.W.
Phone: (206) 782-2027

Spokane
1835 E. 14th Ave.
Phone: (509) 535-2837

Walla Walla
210 Marcus St.
Phone: (509) 527-5488

Wisconsin

Madison
4150 Hiawatha Dr.
Phone: (414) 922-6518

Wauwatosa
7810 Harwood Ave.
Phone: (414) 476-1718

AFRICA
South Africa

Rue de Jacqueline
Somerset West, Cape
Phone: 23187

P.O. Box 238
Sea Point
Phone: 49-6984

P.O. Box 42282
42a Clare Rd.
Fordsburg, Johannesburg
Programs held at:
4631 Lily Ave.
Extension 3 Lenasia

77 Third Rd., Hyde Park
Johannesburg
Phone: 788-5679

ASIA
Israel

Jerusalem
Shtern St. 18, Apt. 17
Kiryat Hayoual
Phone: (02) 417080

Holon
14 Hararee St.
Phone: (03) 846 385

Shenkin 46, 3rd Entrance
Givataim Israel 53304
Phone: 03-281221, 281222
& 281223 (At work)

Philippines

PSC #1 Box 2295
APO San Francisco CA
96286 USA

Australia

Armidale
Puddledock Rd.
Armidale NSW 2350

Bung Bong (Ashram)
P.O. Box 77
Avoca VIC 3467

Canberra
5 Mackellar Crescent
Cook, Canberra ACT 2614
Phone: 512 803 (after
6 pm) & (work) 062 89 6379

Ferny Creek
Wondoora, School Rd
Ferny Creek, Melbourne
3786 VIC

Hawthorn
313 Auburn Rd., Hawthorn
Melbourne VIC 3122
Phone: 82 1985

Kalamunda
54 Kalamunda Rd.
Kalamunda 6076 WA

Melbourne (Ashram)
202 Gore St., Fitzroy
Melbourne VIC 3065
Phone: 419 6950

Narnargoon
Olsen Rd.
N. Narnargoon VIC 3182
Phone: (STD) 059 42 8206

Perth
P.O. Box 158
Cottesloe WA 6011
Programs held at:
9 Ailie St.
Peppermint Grove WA
Phone: 384-4600

Sydney
33 Walker St.
North Sydney NSW 2060
Phone: 929 5431 &
(work) 290 2199

Townsville
5 Morehead St., Flat #1
S. Townsville QLD 4810

Victoria
The Patch
Lot 1 Kallista Emerald Rd.
Victoria 3792
Phone: 756-7009

New Zealand

Auckland
43 A Ranfurly Rd.
Epsom, Auckland

Dunedin
82 Gladstone Rd.
Dunedin, South Island

Canada

Malton
7566 Wrenwood Crescent
Malton ONT L4T 2V7
Phone: (416) 677-3301

Mississauga
6789 Segovia Rd.
Mississauga ONT L5N 1P1
Phone: (416) 826-4512

Ottawa
1300 Pinecrest #1605
Ottawa ONT
Phone: (613) 828-7214

Peterborough
327 Charlotte St.
Peterborough ONT K9J 7C3
Phone: (705) 652-3386

Richmond
10051 4th Ave.
Richmond, B.C.
Phone: (604) 274-9008

Timmins
107 Pine N.
Timmins ONT P4N 6K8
Phone: (705) 267-5776

Toronto
48 Dundonald St.
Toronto ONT M4Y 1K2
Phone: (416) 923-5402

Vancouver
P.O. Box 2990
Vancouver BC V6B 3X4
Phone: (604) 274-9008
& 738-2032

Victoria
1525 McRae Ave.
Phone: (604) 598-2173

EUROPE

England

United Kingdom
91 Taybridge Rd.
London SW 11
Phone: 01-228-0969

Clapham
91 Taybridge Rd.
London SW 11
Phone: 01-228-0969

Eastborne
30 Oakhurst Rd.
Eastborne, Sussex
Phone: Eastborne 37028

East Harling
The Laurels, School Lane
East Harling, Norfolk

Hounslow
15 Ivanhoe Rd.
Hounslow West, Middlesex
Phone: 01-572-3432

Ilford
358 Thorold Rd.
Ilford, Essex
Phone: 01-554-8112
01-552-2200

London
47 Maclean Rd.
Forest Hill, London SE23

82, Livingstone Rd.
Walthamstow
London E17, 9AX
Phone: 01-521-5269

Lowestoft
28 Southwell Rd.
Lowestoft, Suffolk
NR33 ORN
Phone: 05-026-0793

Surrey
Coxhill House
Chobham, Surrey GU24 8AU
Phone: Chobham 8926

France

Bourbourg
12. Ave. General Leclerc
F. 59630
Phone: (16) 20.68.12.91

Nice
30 rue Marceau
Nice 06

Paris
8 rue Freycinet
75116 Paris France
Programs held at:
146 rue Raymond
Losserand
75014 Paris
Phone: 720-8430

33 Ave. du Chateau de Bertin
78400 Chatoux
Programs held at:
14 rue des Sts. Peres
Paris 75007
Phone: 976- 7004

Vesoul
26 Bld. des Allies
Vesoul 70 000

Italy

Rome
Via Monte Del Gatto
Santa Cornelia, Km 3
Phone: (06) 691-3605

Netherlands

Amsterdam
Weteringschans 75
1017 RX Amsterdam
Phone: 020-23.29.92

Soest
Ereprijsstraat 49
Phone: 02155-1717

Spain

Barcelona
Torres y Bages 98-100
1 Piso, Apartment 2

Madrid
Espana
General Pardinas 21
Madrid 1
Phone: 275-3239

Sweden

Malmö
S. Forstadsgat. 102a 3v
S-214 20 Malmö
Phone: (040) 130862

Stockholm
Surbrunnsgatan 6
S-114 21 Stockholm
Phone: (08) 435709

Switzerland

Bern
Brunngasse 54, 3011

Geneva
49. Cure-Baud
1212 Grand-Lancy Geneva
Phone: 94 79 56

West Germany

Darup
Roruperstr. 5

Frankfurt
Fischergasse 5
6050 Offenbach 8
Phone: 0611861260

Munich
Lieberweg 12
D-8000 Munchen 45

Querschied
Am Moosberg 8
(near Saarbrucken)

Mexico

Guadalajara
Av. Americas 1485
Guadalajara 6
Phone: 41-11-35

Mexico City (Ashram)
Apartado 41-890
Mexico 10 DF
Programs held at:
Euclides 9
Colonia Nva. Anzures
Mexico 5 DF
Phone: (905) 545-9375

San Jeronimo
Cerrada Presa 28
San Jeronimo 20
Phone: 595-0980

Tepic
Guerrero 74 Ote.
Tepic, Nayarit
Phone: Tepic 2-27-52

SOUTH AMERICA

Curacao
P.O. Box 807
Curacao Netherlands
Antilles
Phone: 35251, 12213,
&11769

Kwartje 39 Sta. Rosa
Willemstad, Curacao
Netherlands Antilles
Phone: 38880

Trinidad
Union Village, Claxton
Bay
Trinidad West Indies

INDIA

Andhra Pradesh — 1

HYDERABAD

Shree Gurudev Center
Shri Rameshchandra Sanghani,
Shri Bakul Seth,
"Muktashram",
℅, Shri Pravinchandra Modi,
6-3-344 Jubilee Hills,
Hyderabad — 34

Delhi — 3

Siddha Yoga Dham,
Shri Balram Nanda,
Shri Ramesh Kapur,
M-11, Mukta Niwas, Green Park Extn.
New Delhi — 110016

Siddha Yoga Dhyan Kendra,
Shri Santram Vatsya,
K-47, Navin Shahdara, Delhi — 32

Shree Muktanand Dhyan Mandir,
Smt. Urmila Saxena,
Shri Parmama Shanker,
193-E, Dev Nagar,
New Delhi — 110005

Gujarat — 20

AHMEDABAD

Shree Muktanand Dhyan Kendra,
Shri Shirishbhai Desai,
Kum. Bhavna Dhora,
424, Hariniwas, Ashram Road,
Opp. La Gajjar Chamber,
Ahmedabad — 380009

Shree Gurudev Dhyan Kendra,
Shri Niranjan Mehta,
Shri Mahendrabhai Shukla,
15 August Bunglow,
Near Old Police Chawky, Maninagar,
Ahmedabad — 380008

Shree Gurudev Dhyan Mandir,
Smt. Kokila J. Parikh,
5B- Motisagar Society,
Narayan Nagar Road, Paldi,
Ahmedabad — 380007

Shree Gurudev Dhyan Kendra,
Shri Shriram Modak,
A/2 Minita Apartments, Near Swati So-
St. Xaviers High School Road,
Navarangpura, Ahmedabad — 380014

ATUL

Shree Gurudev Dhyan Kendra,
Shri Surendra H. Bhatt,
Shri Ramnikbhai Raval,
Room No — 26, A type Colony,
Atul, Dist.-Valsad

VALSAD (BULSAR)

Shree Gurudev Dhyan Kendra,
Dr. Ratubhai Desai,
Sandhya, Shree Buddha Society,
Halar Road, Valsad

Shree Gurudev Dhyan Mandir,
Shri Dilipbhai Desai,
Smt. Darpanaben Desai,
Hanuman Bhagda, Valsad

Shree Gurudev Dhyan Mandir,
Dr. Jitubhai Parekh,
Kum. Laxmiben Prajapati,
Gangotri, Dhobivad, Valsad

DAHOD

Shree Muktanand Dhyan Kendra,
Shri Gopaldas K. Panchal,
138 'L' Satrasta, Opp. Dayanand Hindi
School, Freelandgang, Dahod
Dist.-Panchmahal

HIMATNAGAR

Shree Gurudev Dhyan Kendra,
Shri Kishorilal Sharma,
Smt. Chandrakantaben Jani,
Kum. Maya Mehta,
Sharma Cottage, Polo Ground,
Near L.I.C. Office, Himatnagar - 383001

KUKARWADA

Siddha Yoga Dham,
Dr. Gangadhar Patel,
Mahant Prempuriji Maharaj,
Kukarwada, Taluke — Vijapur,
Dist.-Mehsana

MOTA JOOJVA

Shree Gurudev Dhyan Kendra,
Shri Babubhai C. Patel,
Shri Dayaji D. Patel,
Shri Thakur D. Patel,
Mota Joojava, Dist.-Valsad

MOTA PONDHA

Shree Gurudev Dhyan Kendra,
Shri Prabhubhai D. Patel,
Mota Pondha, Via- Vapi,
Dist.-Valsad

PARNERA PARDI

Shree Gurudev Dhyan Kendra,
Shri Dolatrai G. Desai,
Parnera Pardi, Dist.-Valsad

SAMANI

Shree Gurudev Dhyan Mandir,
Shri Ghanshyambhai Patel,
Smt. Vidyaben Patel,
At/Post- Samani, Tal.- Amod,
Dist.-Bharuch

SURAT

Siddha Yoga Dham,
Shri Bachubhai Wadiwala,
Smt. Urmila Jariwala,
Shree Nityanand Bhavan,
Kelapith, Surat

UKAI

Shree Gurudev Dhyan Mandir,
Shri Jayantibhai L. Desai,
3A/32 Bhuriwel Colony
Ukai, Dist.-Surat

VAPI

Shree Gurudev Dhyan Mandir,
Shri Krishnarao Dhonde,
Rang Kripa, Zanda Chowk,
Vapi — 396191

DAMAN

Shree Gurudev Dhyan Mandir,
Shri Chunilal Patel,
Bhardwaj Kutir,
Ramji Mandir Compound, Wadi Falia,
Nani Daman, Via- Vapi

SELVASSA

Shree Gurudev Dhyan Mandir,
Shri Madhubhai Patel,
Matruchhaya, Muktanand Marg,
Selvassa, (Dadra Nagar Haveli)

Madhya Pradesh — 3

INDORE

Siddha Yoga Dhyan Kendra,
Shri Basant Kumar Joshi,
89, Emli Bazar (Lal Makan),
Indore — 452002

MHOW

Swami Muktanand Bhakta Mandal,
Shri Balwantrai Sharma,
Bunglow No. L/4A. Rly. Colony,
Mhow, Dist. Indore

RATLAM

Shree Sadguru Bhakta Mandal,
Shri Chunilal Rathod,
Shri Jaisinh S. Pol,
Sadguru Dhyan Kutir,
Nagar Nigam Colony, Block No. 316,
Gandhi Nagar, Ratlam

Maharashtra — 14

AURANGABAD

Muktanand Dhyan Kendra,
Shri B.S. Patil,
Smt. Rajani Patil,
Mukteswari, Prabhat Colony,
Aurangabad

BARAMATI

Shree Gurudev Dhyan Kendra,
Smt. Lila Kale,
Kale Wada, Baramati,
Dist.-Poona

BHUSAWAL

Shree Gurudev Mandir,
Shri Sudhir Rajabhao Kulkarni,
Muktanand Bhavan, Ram Mandir
Bhusawal, Dist.-Jalgaon

BOMBAY

Siddha Yoga Dhyan Kendra,
Kum. Bharati Dicholkar,
New Liberty Co. Op. Housing Society
Guru Kripa, Block No. 9,
Liberty Garden Cross Road No. 4,
Malad, Bombay — 400065

Nityamukta Siddha Yoga Dham,
Shri Pranubhai Desai,
A/17 Madhav Apartments,
Shimpoli, Borivli, (West) Bombay

Siddha Yoga Dhyan Kendra,
Kum. Lalita Parasarmani,
Guru Chhaya, 62/1 Mulund Colony,
Mulund, Bombay — 400082

DOMBIVALI

Shree Sadguru Muktanand
Swadhyaya Mandal,
Shri Vasantrao Malpathak,
Khot Kaparekar Bldg.,
Agarkar Road, Dombivali (East)
Dist.-Thana

FAIZPUR

Shree Gurudev Dhyan Mandir,
Shri Shamlal Varma,
Shri Rajendrakumar Varma,
Faizpur, Dist.-Jalgaon

KOLHAPUR

Siddha Yoga Dhyan Kendra,
Smt. Jayashree Kori,
Smt. Vijaya D. Ligade,
Prabha, Rajarampuri,
14th Street, Kolhapur — 416001

MANMAD

Shree Gurudev Dhyan Kendra,
Smt. Kusumatai D. Deshmukh,
Railway Colony, R.B. 2-629A,
Yeola Road, Manmad

NAGPUR

Siddha Yoga Dhyan Kendra,
Shri Vasantrao Ghonge,
Mukta Niwas, Gopalnagar,
Nagpur — 440010

POONA

Shree Gurudev Dhyan Mandir,
Prof. G. H. Sujan,
44 Connought House,
12 Sadhu Vasvani Road,
Poona — 411001

Siddha Yoga Dhyan Mandir,
Smt. Pragna Trivedi,
"Kamal", 479/2 Harekrishna Path,
Shivaji Nagar, Poona — 411016

SAPTASHRING

Shree Saptashring Gurudev Ashram,
Swami Prakashanand Saraswati,
Saptashring Gadh,
Post- Nanduri, Tal.-Kalvan,
Dist.-Nasik,
(Residential Ashram)

Rajasthan — 4

JAIPUR

Shree Muktanand Dhyan Mandir,
Smt. Bhagvati Mukta,
B-222, Janata Colony, Agra Road,
Jaipur — 302008

Shree Muktanand Dhyan Mandir,
Shri Nandkishor Varma,
Shree Muktanand Niketan,
Gator Road, Brahmapuri,
Jaipur — 302002

NAGAUR

Siddha Yoga Dhyan Kendra,
Shri Sitaram Soni,
Katharia Bazar, Nagaur

TONK

Shree Muktanand Dhyan Mandir,
Shri Gopalsimh Bhati,
Abdul Qayum's House,
Barmor Darwaja, Tonk

Uttar Pradesh — 2

AGRA

Siddah Yoga Dhyan Kendra,
Dr. Chandrapal Singh,
Ram Niwas, 32 Heerabag Colony,
Swamibag, Agra — 282005

TENTI GAON

Shree Muktanand Dhyan Kendra,
Shri Ramshankar Lavania,
At/Post- Tenti Gaon, Dist.-Mathura

West Bangal — 2

CALCUTTA

Muktanand Dhyan Kendra,
Shri Balkrishna Agarwal,
11 Pollack Street, 1st Floor,
Room No.-3, Calcutta — 700001

Muktanand Dhyan Kendra,
Smt. Shukla Lal,
Shri Shadi Lal,
Flat No. 15, 8th Floor,
8-B, Alipur Road, Calcutta - 700027

OTHER PUBLICATIONS

By Swami Muktananda

Play Of Consciousness Muktananda's Spiritual Autobiography
Satsang With Baba (Three Volumes) Questions and Answers
Getting Rid Of What You Haven't Got Introductory Talks
Muktananda-Selected Essays Edited by Paul Zweig
Light On The Path Essays On Siddha Yoga
Sadgurunath Maharaj Ki Jaya Photos and Essays Of The 1970 Australian Tour
Siddha Meditation Commentaries On The Shiva Sutras
Mukteshwari I & II Aphorisms
So'ham Japa Short Essay On The So'ham Mantra
Ashram Dharma Essay On Ashram Life
A Book For The Mind Aphorisms On The Mind
I Love You Aphorisms On Love
What Is An Intensive? Description of Muktananda's 2-day program
Bhagawan Nityananda Biography Of Muktananda's Guru, Swami Nityananda

About Swami Muktananda

Swami Muktananda Paramahansa By Amma — Muktananda's Biography
Sadhana Photographic Essay of Muktananda's Spiritual Practice
Muktananda Siddha Guru By Shankar

Other Books

Introduction To Kashmir Shaivism
Siddha Cooking Cookbook
Nectar Of Chanting Sanskrit Chants Transliterated and Translated

Publications

Muktananda Siddha Path Monthly Magazine of S.Y.D.A. Foundation
Shree Gurudev Ashram Newsletter Monthly Newsletter From India
Shree Gurudev-Vani Annual Journal By Devotees

Books Available In Other Languages

Play Of Consciousness (French, German, Italian & Spanish)
Nectar Of Chanting (French & German)
So'ham Japa (French & German)

(Most of Swami Muktananda's books are also available in Hindi)

These books and Publications are distributed by S.Y.D.A. Foundation and are also available at Centers and Ashrams and by selected bookstores throughout the world. For further information, contact: S.Y.D.A. Foundation, P.O. Box 11071, Oakland, California 94611, U.S.A., Phone (415) 655-8677